PRESBYTERIAN BELIEFS
Revised Edition

Also by Donald K. McKim

PRESBYTERIAN BELIEFS
A Brief Introduction

Revised Edition

Donald K. McKim

WESTMINSTER
JOHN KNOX PRESS
LOUISVILLE • KENTUCKY

Revised edition
Published by Westminster John Knox Press
Louisville, Kentucky

17 18 19 20 21 22 23 24 25 26—10 9 8 7 6 5 4 3 2 1

Book design by Sharon Adams
Cover design by Allison Taylor

Library of Congress Cataloging-in-Publication Data

Names: McKim, Donald K., author.
Title: Presbyterian beliefs : a brief introduction / Donald K. McKim.
Description: Revised edition. | Louisville, KY : Westminster John
 Knox Press, 2017. | Includes bibliographical references. |
Identifiers: LCCN 2017006620 (print) | LCCN 2017029396 (ebook) |
 ISBN 9781611648225 (ebk.) | ISBN 9780664263270 (pbk. : alk. paper)
Subjects: LCSH: Presbyterian Church--Doctrines.
Classification: LCC BX9175.3 (ebook) | LCC BX9175.3 .M35 2017
 (print) | DDC 285/.137--dc23
LC record available at https://lccn.loc.gov/2017006620

Most Westminster John Knox Press books are available at special quantity discounts when purchased in bulk by corporations, organizations, and special-interest groups. For more information, please e-mail SpecialSales@wjkbooks.com.

To my family:

LindaJo
Stephen and Caroline, Maddie, Annie, and Jack
Karl and Lauren

With deepest love and gratitude

Contents

Preface to the Revised Edition

When this book was published in 2003, it joined my *Introducing the Reformed Faith* as a source for laity, seminary students, and pastors to study and reflect on our Reformed and Presbyterian theology. Then followed *Presbyterian Questions, Presbyterian Answers*; *More Presbyterian Questions, More Presbyterian Answers*; and *Presbyterian Faith That Lives Today*, along with other further resources for those interested in understanding Presbyterian beliefs.

Recent changes in the *Book of Confessions* and the *Book of Order* of the Presbyterian Church in the United States of America (PC(USA)) have meant that it is useful to update books to reflect the addition of the Confession of Belhar to the *Book of Confessions* and present understandings and terminology in the *Book of Order*. Some other modifications have been made along the way in *Presbyterian Beliefs*. For superb help and suggestions about what to adjust here, I would like to thank David Maxwell of Westminster John Knox Press. His comments have been very valuable. He also has prepared some case study questions to enhance the use of this book. My thanks also go to David Dobson and Julie Tonini of the press for their support and splendid work.

The need for these modifications highlights that change is a feature of our Christian faith and that Presbyterian understandings and expressions, particularly in the PC(USA) do take place—by the leading of the Spirit of God, we believe. A theological way of understanding "change" is to see change as God moving us from where we are to where God wants us to be. Even when the changes seem relatively small, they still represent this action of God's guiding providence. As it is in the church's life, so it is in our own lives.

Changes in my life in these last years have led my beloved wife, LindaJo, and me to our sons' spouses, and we have welcomed grandchildren to our family. We now rejoice in life with Stephen and Caroline and their children, Maddie, Annie, and Jack; as well as with Karl and Lauren. These blessed members of the family that God has given lead me to praise, thanks, and gratitude. To them, this book is lovingly dedicated.

Changes come, within the church and in our own experience. As we move along, my hope is that these books will continue to benefit the church. May they be a blessing to all who seek further understanding and nurture in their lives of faith. May we all seek to "grow in the grace and knowledge of our Lord and Savior Jesus Christ" (2 Pet. 3:18).

Donald K. McKim
Germantown, Tennessee
Advent 2016

Preface to the First Edition

I am a Presbyterian. I have written this book out of a deep love for Presbyterian theology and the beliefs that have shaped generations of Presbyterians throughout the world. My desire is to communicate the major elements of Presbyterian beliefs as simply and clearly as possible.

This book has chapters titled with theological words. They are some of the vocabulary of Christian—and Presbyterian—theology. My goal is to unpack these words and to say as plainly as possible what Presbyterians believe about these terms.

Those who have studied Presbyterian theology will know it is impossible to do full justice to all the varieties of viewpoints on theological issues that one finds among Presbyterians. Every chapter here can be expanded greatly. I have quoted directly from only two theological sources: the *Book of Confessions* of the Presbyterian Church (U.S.A.) (cited as *BC*) and the *Institutes of the Christian Religion,* written in the sixteenth century by John Calvin (cited as *Institutes*). Many other sources could be used. But for simplicity's sake and because these two are important, I have used only them.

This book will not answer all your questions about Presbyterian beliefs. I trust it will answer some. I hope it will raise others. If it does, there are a number of resources listed as "For Further Study" in the back of the book that can point the way to help you think about these further issues.

The basics of the chapters that follow have been shared in several Presbyterian churches. I would like to thank the sessions, people, and pastors of First Presbyterian Church, Greenville, Mississippi, and Dr. Emett Barfield; First Presbyterian Church, Helena, Arkansas, and the Rev. Richard Goodman; as well as Trinity Presbyterian Church, Berwyn, Pennsylvania—where I have gratefully served as interim pastor—and Dr. Jay Wilkins. I would also like to thank the Rev. Betty Meadows and the Committee of the Synod of Living Waters Congregational Development Conference for the opportunity to present much of this material to this conference.

I dedicate this book to my family—LindaJo, Stephen, and Karl. Their love and support bring meaning and abundant joy to my life.

Donald K. McKim
Germantown, Tennessee
September 11, 2002

Introduction

This is a book for those interested in Presbyterian beliefs. Perhaps you are considering joining a Presbyterian church. Perhaps you have always heard of "Presbyterians" and have wondered what views these people hold. Or perhaps you have been a lifelong Presbyterian—baptized, confirmed, even married in a Presbyterian church—and now it is time to examine more closely what Presbyterians believe.

Theological beliefs have always been important to Presbyterians. This has been good in that it has given us a highly developed theology that expresses clearly what is believed about a whole host of topics. We have confessions of faith, theological books, and thousands of pages to articulate what theological beliefs Presbyterians hold dear. On the other hand, sometimes our concerns for scrupulous theology have made Presbyterians lose sight of broader visions or have caused splits or breaks in the body of Christ, the church. There's a bit of a sting in the story of two Presbyterians who were marooned on an island: one started the "First Presbyterian Church" and the other started the "Second Presbyterian Church." Meticulous concerns for theology can sometimes make us neglect other important issues like care and love for others.

This book is to introduce Presbyterian beliefs in a simple and straightforward way. It is pretty much "straight theology"—a concise statement of the major theological viewpoints that Presbyterians hold.

Yet we should also note that as the little story of the two Presbyterians suggests, there are varieties within "Presbyterian" beliefs. This has always been the case, as long as there have been "Presbyterians." Today in the United States there are a number of church bodies that call themselves "Presbyterian." These churches hold many theological beliefs in common—enough to make them "Presbyterian." Yet they are often distinctive because of some particular beliefs or emphases that set them apart from others who hold the name "Presbyterian." Often this relates to the particular confession of faith (or "creed") that a church regards as authoritative. Many Presbyterian churches regard the Westminster Confession of Faith (1647) as the best statement of Presbyterian belief. The largest Presbyterian denomination in the United States, the Presbyterian Church (U.S.A.), has a *Book of Confessions* as its standard for what to believe. These are creeds and confessions of faith that span history from the early church period up to the end of the twentieth century. So this wider expanse of theological statements naturally introduces more variety and variations into the Presbyterian belief tapestry.

Presbyterians belong to the Reformed theological tradition. When we join a Presbyterian church, we enter a family. It is a family with an impressive genealogy. It is a family that traces its origins to Christian believers who lived in Europe during the sixteenth century. These were Christians who followed the views of several significant theologians who lived during and after the time Martin Luther began what is commonly called the "Protestant Reformation." When Luther questioned certain teachings of the dominant Roman Catholic Church in 1517, a revolution of reformation swept through Europe. Those theologians who followed Luther in rejecting Roman Catholic theology but who went on to develop theological views different from Luther's were called "Reformed" theologians. Those who followed these "Reformed" writers believed these theologians had provided the most compelling ways of reading the Holy Scriptures and understanding who God is, what Jesus Christ has done, and how God wants Christian people to live in the church. The theologian regarded most highly was John Calvin (1509–64), who spent most of his ministry in Geneva, Switzerland. Other important theologians were Huldrych Zwingli (1484–1531) and Zwingli's successor as minister in Zurich, Heinrich Bullinger (1504–75). The theological understandings these and other Reformed theologians promoted were distinguished from other theological groups, including the Lutherans—who followed the views of Luther—and the Anabaptists—who are the ancestors of our modern-day Baptists and Pentecostals. They got the name "Reformed" because they wanted to reform God's church on the basis of Scripture.

Reformed theology and the Reformed tradition spread from Calvin's Geneva throughout Switzerland, France, and Germany and into the Low Countries during the next decades. Important emigration led to the Reformed faith—as a way of understanding the Scriptures and as a theological belief system—being spread throughout the world. Today there are Reformed Christians all over the globe. In America, streams of the Reformed tradition came from England, Scotland, and the Netherlands. The establishment of American Presbyterianism at the end of the eighteenth century came through the efforts of thousands of Christian believers who understood themselves as Reformed Christians.

In the United States today, the Reformed faith is shared by a number of denominations. The Reformed Church in America and the Christian Reformed Church, for example, reflect the legacy and influence of the Dutch Reformed settlers in America. The United Church of Christ has emerged from New England Puritan settlers who embraced Reformed theology but organized their churches on a congregational model. They were known as Congregationalists. In this polity, each individual congregation is essentially autonomous and makes its own decisions without the oversight of a wider body. Many of the various "Presbyterian" denominations in the United States trace their roots to European church bodies. These churches are rooted in Reformed theology and are organized on a "presbyterian" model of church government.

Though we speak of the Reformed tradition and the Reformed faith, it is important to realize that this is a tradition and a faith that has had a variety of ways of expressing itself theologically. Basic insights are found in the writings of Calvin, particularly his classic *Institutes of the Christian Religion* (editions from 1536 to 1560). This book has been like a spine, or backbone, for Reformed theology. But other Reformed theologians have formulated their understandings in differing ways. In addition, it has been characteristic of Reformed Christians wherever they have been to express their faith through the construction of confessions of faith. These "creeds" are formulations of what believers understand the Scriptures to teach on various theological doctrines. These many confessions from the Reformed heritage also exhibit various ways of understanding and expressing Christian doctrines or teachings. Even the order with which the doctrines are dealt is different from confession to confession. So we have variety within the Reformed faith.

Presbyterianism is one part of the Reformed theological tradition. Most directly, Presbyterianism gets its name from the ways in which its churches are governed. A "presbyterian" system of church government or polity features a "presbytery" as a key governing body, now called a council. Local churches are governed by church sessions, which are composed of "elders" who are elected by the congregation (in the New Testament, the Greek word *presbyteros*—from which "Presbyterian" is derived—means "elder"). A number of churches in a particular geographical area constitute a presbytery. The presbytery is made up of elected representatives (clergy and laity) from the regional churches. A number of presbyteries in a particular region constitute a "synod," and all the synods jointly constitute the "General Assembly," which is the highest council of the church. It's often pointed out that governing structures of the United States mirror Presbyterian church government. There are local city governments, county governments, state governments, and then the national or federal government. Presbyterianism is a representative system where those who serve in the councils are elected. The main unit beyond the local church is the presbytery. Thus the name "Presbyterian" emerges.

"Presbyterian theology" refers to what Presbyterians believe about Christian theology. A definable "shape" to Presbyterian theology can be distinguished, both historically and among contemporary Presbyterians. The confessions of faith that have been part of the Reformed and Presbyterian heritage have been chief expressions of Reformed or Presbyterian beliefs. So have the writings of those theologians who have self-consciously considered themselves to be "Reformed" theologians.

The chapters that follow outline some major emphases of the Reformed faith on a number of important Christian doctrines. In many cases, Presbyterians share key insights with other Christians and other expressions of Christian doctrines. Basic beliefs in God, Jesus Christ, and the Holy Spirit are held in common with all other Christians. These are our significant, ecumenical beliefs that unite us as sisters and brothers in Christ with the whole Christian church, worldwide. These common affirmations of unity are the "big picture." We hold much more in common with other Christians than we hold as distinctively "Presbyterian" beliefs.

But as we move on into the details of Christian doctrine, we find that Presbyterian theology and Reformed confessions have spoken with distinctive accents and with particular emphases. These distinctives help set our Presbyterian understandings apart from other theological views—for example, Roman Catholic, Lutheran, Methodist, or Baptist views. Today we tend to emphasize commonalities in our Christian faith and experience. These are tremendously important. But when it comes to understanding what makes us distinctively or particularly or especially "Presbyterian" Christians, we can turn to these Reformed perspectives that give us our unique blend of theological understandings.

To help us get handles on some of these, we will examine a number of Christian doctrines in the following chapters. Broadly, we will first look at "The God Who Reveals, Creates, and Guides." Here we will consider the doctrines of God's revelation in Scripture, the Trinity, creation, and providence. A second segment will consider "The Christ Who Saves People like Us." Here our focus will be on the doctrines of humanity, sin, the person and work of Christ, the Holy Spirit, election and predestination, and salvation by grace. In the third section our attention will be on "The Church, Where Faith Begins, Is Nourished, and Grows." Here we will look at the doctrines of the church, the Christian life, and the future life.

Presbyterian belief is one way of being a Christian believer. It is not the only way. It may not even be the best way. But Presbyterians have taken their theological beliefs seriously because they take God seriously. Whenever we make any statement at all about God, we are being a theologian. Presbyterian theology is one way of helping us understand who God is and what God has done in human history, on the basis of God's communication to humanity through Scripture. The following "Presbyterian primer" introduces us to one way of doing theology and one way of understanding God's wonderful, glorious gospel, centered in Jesus Christ our Lord.

PART I

The God Who Reveals, Creates, and Guides

1

Revelation

*H*ow can we know God? This is one of life's most basic questions. Perhaps there is no God. Perhaps there is. If there is not a God, then we don't need to worry about this question. If there is a God, and if we are interested in finding out anything about this God, then we wonder: How can we know God?

One thing seems obvious. If there is a God, that is, a God who is not immediately apparent to our senses or our intelligence, then we need a way to know God that is something more than what we ourselves can invent or concoct. We need a way of knowing God that enables us to know that which is beyond us or greater than us — to know God. This means of knowing must be a method that we can trust. It must be a method that provides truth about God while at the same time being a way that we can understand and comprehend. This way of knowing God needs to be a way that is available to all people. It should not be a "secret knowledge" or the private preserve of an elite group of persons. The knowledge of God should be open universally to all persons. It should be able to be apprehended by all, even if — and it seems this is the case, based on our experiences — not all persons accept this knowledge, or trust it, or believe it. In short, we need a way for the knowledge of God to be made known to us.

Since we are limited human beings who recognize our restrictions and boundaries as humans, if we are to gain any valid knowledge of God, it would seem that God must impart this knowledge to us. Since the idea of a "god" has been around since the beginning of human history (we assume), and since persons throughout history have not agreed on who this God is or what this God is like (this is evident from the great number of religions and philosophies that have been part of human experience through the centuries), then it is clear that human knowledge, reason, or experience alone cannot come to a common agreement on the knowledge of God. Every religion or philosophy has its own teachings about who "God" is or what "God" is like. This points us to the conclusion that if there is a God, then true and valid knowledge about this God can only be obtained if that God chooses to be revealed. If this were not so, we would never know anything about God at all. If God were not revealed—in some way, somehow—we would have to remain forever silent about God.

This seems obvious, doesn't it? If God is revealed, it is God who must do the revealing. Humans cannot storm up to the gates of heaven, peel away the clouds, and peer into the face of God! There's no way that can happen! If we are ever to "see the face of God," it is God who must reveal that face. God is the one who is revealed; and God is the one who must do the revealing. God must make the first move.

> If God is revealed, it is God who must do the revealing. Humans cannot storm up to the gates of heaven, peel away the clouds, and peer into the face of God!

This is one of the basic assumptions of Christian faith. We believe that God takes the initiative and chooses to be revealed or communicate with humanity. When we speak of God revealing God's self to us, we are referring theologically to the doctrine of revelation. "Revelation" means an "uncovering," a making known that which is hidden. God is unknown to humans; God is hidden from us and the whole human race. Since we cannot see God, or hear God, or perceive God with our senses, many people assume that God does not exist. But Christians affirm that while "no one has ever seen God" (John 1:18; 1 John 4:12), God is real. God is active and God has—astonishingly—chosen to be revealed to humanity and to communicate with the human race. This is the doctrine of revelation.

The doctrine of revelation is basic and fundamental to all Christian theology. Without it, there could be no theology or "study of God." Without God's revealing, we would know nothing of God at all. Many of the world's great religions speak about finding a way to God. How do humans discover the path to the divine? Christianity affirms, however, that God has found the way to humanity and has chosen to be made known to the created creatures of this world.

General Revelation

Christians have distinguished between General or Natural Revelation and Special Revelation. General revelation refers to a knowledge of God that can be conveyed in nature or through human reason. If we look at the world and say: "Ah, such a creation must have a creator; it couldn't just come into being all by itself," or look at human beings and think: "Ah, we are so marvelously made, so intricate, so complex—we couldn't have just evolved all by ourselves"—then we are in the realm of "natural" or "general" revelation. General revelation is not communicated in words. Rather, it is the perception arrived at by our own human means—whatever they may be—that there must be a "God" who has caused the world and human beings to exist.

Some Reformed theologians have upheld a revelation of God in nature. They have appealed to certain scriptural passages, such as the text: "The heavens are telling the glory of God; and the firmament proclaims his handiwork" (Ps. 19:1). The text seems to say that if we look around us, we see all creation and that creation "tells" or "declares" to us "the glory of God"—or the fact that there is a God behind it all.

The question is, however, whether this perception of nature is adequate to reveal God. Can we know that there is a God by observing nature? Will all of us come to the same conclusion about the reality of God based on our perceptions of the world around us? Since everyone in the world does not appear to believe in a "God" based on the assessment of nature around us, it seems that natural or general revelation is not sufficient in itself to convince people of the reality of God's existence. Even more, it does not at all indicate the nature or character of God or what God may have done in human history.

Other Reformed theologians, however, have pointed out that this verse from the Psalms was written to a group of people who already believed in God. The Hebrews believed God existed and was the creator of all things. This is apparent from the very first verse of the Hebrew Bible (Gen. 1:1). So it would be natural to say to these people that if you look at the world around you, you will see the glory of God: in the heavens as well as the earth. These theologians say that there is a "general revelation" of God in nature—not for the unbelievers, but for the believers. We come to a knowledge of God. After we do, then, there exists for us an amazing "general" or "natural" revelation around us. When those who already believe in God observe nature or the wonders of human life, they see the glory of God before their eyes.

But if there is not a "general revelation" in nature—or even if there is—will this be a sufficient source for our knowledge of God? Will we know all there is to know about God, or all we need to know about God, simply by looking around us and using our reason, perhaps, to deduce the existence of a God behind it all?

Special Revelation

Christian theologians have been unanimous in saying that, even if there is a "general revelation," that does not tell us all we need to know about God. There are things we need to know about God that we will never be able to deduce from nature or from the reasoning powers of our minds. We need a "special revelation." We need a revelation that tells us special things, gives us a special knowledge of God beyond what we could ever know by our human reason or by observing the world around us.

Scripture. We believe that this special revelation is what we have in the Scriptures, or the Bible. The Bible is God's "special revelation" in that it conveys a knowledge of God we would not be able to attain in any other way or through any other means.

The Scriptures are called the "Word of God." They are referred to in this way because it is through the Scriptures that God speaks.

The Westminster Confession of Faith, an important Reformed confession written by English Puritans during the English Civil War in the seventeenth century, referred to the Scriptures as "the Word of God written" (*BC* 6.002). The Scriptures are the means or the medium through which God communicates a knowledge of God. The Scriptures are the place to turn to learn of God in a complete and unique and authoritative manner. The Scriptures convey the nature of God—who God is and what God does. The Scriptures are the story of God's activities in the created world.

> The Bible is God's "special revelation" in that it conveys a knowledge of God we would not be able to attain in any other way, or through any other means.

Through the Hebrew Scriptures we see what the people of faith in the nation of Israel believed God was doing in what we call the Old Testament. The Old Testament reveals God's actions in Israel's history and in choosing Israel to be a special people to carry out the divine purposes in this world. It tells us the story of Israel's faith. We read of God's creation of the world and humans, of God entering into a covenant relationship with Abraham and Sarah (Gen. 12) to establish what would become the nation of Israel to be a "light to the nations" (Isa. 42:6), to be God's servant people. The Old Testament recounts Israel's history from the perspective of its faith, and especially God's astounding liberation and deliverance of the people of Israel from their slavery in Egypt (Exod. 20:2) and the revelation of the Law of God in the Ten Commandments to show Israel how God wanted them to live as covenant people (Exod. 20:1–17).

In the New Testament, we see the culmination or climax of God's divine revelation in the person of Jesus of Nazareth, the One the early Christian church called Jesus the Christ ("Messiah"). Israel anticipated that God would send a messiah to establish peace and justice on the earth. Christians believe that God's Messiah has come in the person of Jesus of Nazareth (Acts 2:36; 3:20; 5:42). We believe the New Testament is also God's divine self-communication, a divine revelation that takes its ultimate shape in the person of Jesus Christ, who Christians believe is the Son of God (Rom. 1:4; 2 Cor. 1:19).

In common with other theological traditions, Presbyterians have emphasized the authority of Scripture. God is revealed in the Scriptures. The Scriptures are God's "special revelation," the source of our knowledge of God. In the Bible, we encounter God as in no other place. Thus the Scriptures have authority for us—because they are the basis for our knowledge of God. We believe and obey the Scriptures because they are the unique source of our knowledge about God. The Bible is distinctive among all other books and literature, because it is in and through the Scriptures that God speaks. Most clearly, God has spoken in the person of Jesus Christ.

> In the Bible, we encounter God as in no other place. Thus the Scriptures have authority for us—because they are the basis for our knowledge of God.

To say the Bible is authoritative or that the Scriptures are unique does not answer all our questions. We will want to know not only what to believe about God but also how God wants us to live. We will need to know what values to adopt in life or what the basis for our decisions should be. This means there will always be the need to interpret the Scriptures, to use all the resources in our reach that can help us understand what the Bible means and what the meanings of the Scriptures are for our own situations. It is important to affirm the authority of Scripture. But it is also important to take the next steps and be serious about interpreting the Bible so that it can play an authoritative role in our Christian lives.

While Presbyterians believe that the Scriptures are inspired by God, diverse viewpoints are found here. But a common conviction remains: God is the one who is, in some sense, "behind" the Scriptures. The writers wrote. Yet the Holy Spirit was somehow involved in the writing. Just how the Spirit was at work is a contested question. Did the Spirit guide the writing of each word of Scripture so that the writers were more or less secretaries or stenographers? Did God suggest the thoughts that writers wrote in their own words? Or does God's Spirit simply use the words that were written by the authors on their own—use them as witnesses to God's revelation in Jesus Christ? In the Reformed tradition, we find representatives of each of these three views. Some "good Presbyterians" believe each of these positions. But all of them affirm that the Scriptures are "inspired." The Bible is unique because in and through the Scriptures God speaks in a special way.

The Scriptures are God's divine revelation. They are the "Word of God written." They are inspired by God and are authoritative for our lives of faith—for what we believe and what we do. We also believe it is the Holy Spirit who is intimately connected with the Scriptures. The Spirit inspired the Scripture writers and those who shaped the biblical documents. The Spirit illuminates the Scriptures for us, meaning that the Holy Spirit of God is the One who enlightens us and convinces us that the Scriptures are God's Word. Through the Spirit we are enabled to perceive God in the Scriptures. Through special revelation in Scripture, God is communicated to us. God's will and purposes for our lives are made known.

The Holy Spirit also helps us interpret the Bible. Presbyterian Christians believe we should use all the tools we have to help us understand the Bible. There are various ways of approaching the Bible, using the insights of what is called "biblical criticism." This does not mean a "criticism" that "criticizes," or devalues, the Bible. Instead it means a way of evaluating the biblical writings. We study the language of the Scriptures, their backgrounds, the culture in which they were written, their literary forms, the communities that first read the Scriptures—all these dimensions. We study, using the best resources we have, in order to be as well equipped as possible to hear God speaking to us in the Scriptures.

But at the same time we also trust and rely on the Holy Spirit to guide us in our interpretation. We pray when we read the Bible. We pray for God to give the Spirit to us, to lead us into God's truth, and to help us understand what God would have us know. We do not trust our own insights alone. We do trust that God will use our insights and, by means of the Spirit, will speak to us through the inspired Scripture to convey to us God's Word for us today. We are able to "hear," or perceive, God's Holy Spirit speaking through the Scriptures in many ways. One of the best ways is in the community of other believers, the church. Where the Scriptures are studied, preached, and taught, the Holy Spirit can work and give us the insights we need. God's Word and God's Spirit go together. The Spirit helps us interpret the Scriptures, and the Scriptures are the means God uses to guide us, through the Holy Spirit.

So the Scriptures are God's "special revelation." In the Bible, God speaks to us as in no other place. As we move along to discuss what Presbyterians believe, we will rely on the Bible as our authoritative source. Reformed and Presbyterian theology through the centuries has always been based on Scripture as its starting point. Our theological statements are statements drawn from what we believe the Scriptures teach. When we study theology and confess our faith, we do so on the basis of God's self-revelation in the Scriptures. This is why the Bible has such a central place in our churches and in our own lives. We read and study the Scriptures to understand who God is, what God has done, and how God wants us to live. Through Scripture we gain a knowledge of God that is reliable and authoritative. We know God through the Scriptures as God speaks to us by Word and Spirit. When we know God, we love God and seek to obey God's will for our lives. This is why the psalmist said that God's word is "a lamp to my feet and a light to my path" (Ps. 119:105).

Questions for Discussion

1. What "evidence" do you see for the existence of God around you?
2. Why is "special revelation" important?
3. Why is the Bible, written in ancient times, able to be significant for us today?
4. What do we mean by the "authority" of Scripture?
5. Why is it important to believe that we have a trustworthy Bible?

Trinity

Our Common Faith

*P*resbyterian Christians, with other Christians, confess our faith in one God in three persons: Father, Son, and Holy Spirit. This is the Christian doctrine of the Trinity. We worship one God, whom we know as three distinct persons. These three persons are called Father, Son, and Holy Spirit. They are not three distinct and separate persons in the sense of being three individuals, each one doing a job cut off and separate from the others. Rather, Father, Son, and Holy Spirit are intimately related with each other. "One God in three persons" is what the church confesses. And we confess it as a mystery. We do not and cannot understand how this can be. But we believe that there is one personal God and that this God lives and works in three different ways at the same time. Now let's try to unpack this a bit.

Like ancient Israel and the whole Old Testament, we confess our faith in one God. Basic to Old Testament faith was the affirmation: "Hear, O Israel: The LORD is our God, the LORD alone" (Deut. 6:4). Israel was to worship and serve the "one" God, who alone is the supreme being. Christians are not "polytheists," which means belief in many gods. Like Israel, we are "monotheists"—we believe in one God. This God is a personal God. We do not worship nature, or some force, or some impersonal being. We worship a God whom we can know and love and a God who can know and love us. We believe in one personal God.

We also believe this God lives and works in three different ways at the same time. The earliest Christians could not separate their belief in God from the man Jesus of Nazareth. Jesus of Nazareth was unique in their experience. In Jesus, early followers found that they experienced God. Jesus acted as God acts. Jesus did things that only God could do. Jesus was, the early Christians came to believe, "God with us" ("Emmanuel," Matt. 1:23). When we meet this human being Jesus, we meet God. The church through the early centuries recognized that Jesus was God; yet he was also distinct from the God of the Old Testament. For this man Jesus was also a truly human person. He prayed to God (John 17), he relied on God (Mark 14:35–36), he lived his life in trustful obedience to God (John 4:34). So we have the two dimensions here. Jesus, the early Christians believed, *was* God; yet he was also distinct *from* God.

In a similar way, early Christians could not separate their belief in God or their belief in Jesus from their experience of the Holy Spirit. At Pentecost, the Holy Spirit came upon the church in great power (Acts 2). Those early Christians knew that through that Spirit they were experiencing God's power. They called the Spirit "Lord" (2 Cor. 3:17–18) and "God" (Acts 5:3–4). They found as they lived their lives as followers of Jesus Christ that the Holy Spirit was their companion. The Spirit is personal (Rom. 8:14, 16; Eph. 4:30). The Spirit lived in their lives and did lead them into the deep truths of faith, just as Jesus said (John 16:13). This Spirit, they realized, was also distinct from God and from Jesus, yet, just as surely, they believed that in the Spirit they also encountered God.

Through the early centuries, the Christian church wrestled with trying to find words and language that were adequate to confess its belief in God. God is "one," yet God is "three." There is a unity in God, yet also a "trinity"—the term that came to be used. The church eventually confessed its faith that there is "one God in three persons." The one personal God lives and works in three different ways at the same time. It is important to realize that this God works in three different ways "at the same time"—because this assures us that this one God is not just "pretending" to be someone else when we encounter Jesus Christ or the Holy Spirit. Jesus and the Spirit are truly God. They are truly God at the same time as God the Father is God.

One of the views the early church rejected and called heresy was called "modalism." This means that God appeared in three different "modes" or stages. In the Old Testament, there was God the Father; then in the New Testament there was God the Son; and then, after Pentecost, there was God the Holy Spirit. So, like a soap opera with its cast of characters, God was gradually "unfolding" in three different characters or modes. Sometimes we hear the Trin-

> The church eventually confessed its faith that there is "one God in three Persons." The one personal God lives and works in three different ways at the same time.

ity explained by saying that God is like H_2O. H_2O exists in three different forms: solid, liquid, and gas. As a solid it is ice, as a liquid it is water, as a gas it is water vapor. So God as Trinity is said to exist in these three different forms, or modes. But the church rejected this view as a heresy. For there is only one God, who is one God in three persons—and each of these persons is always and forever God. They do not exist as three different modes at different times in history—like the solid, or liquid, or gas. No. God works as three persons at the same time, ever and always. The Trinity as Father, Son, and Holy Spirit is one God, eternally.

The three members, or persons, of the Trinity are fully equal with each other. This too was an important point for early Christians. One of the views that the early church rejected was called "subordinationism." This was the view that the Son and the Spirit were "less" than God the Father. They were "subordinate," in the sense of not being equal to or "fully" God. Those who believed this were trying to safeguard the "unity" of God. God is one. God cannot share God's self or essence with other beings. So the Son and Spirit must be less divine than the Father.

The church rejected this view because it did not faithfully represent what the church believed the New Testament teaches. If subordinationism were true, then neither the Son nor the Spirit would be fully divine. This would mean that Jesus Christ could not be fully God, that God did not enter into the world fully in the person of Jesus Christ to bring about salvation. It would mean that the Holy Spirit is not fully God, and so God is not altogether with the church in the presence of the Spirit, leading and guiding the church and the lives of individual Christians.

So the early church rejected "modalism" and "subordination-ism" to affirm the full equality of the Father, Son, and Holy Spirit. Eventually the language of Greek philosophy was employed to try to capture this truth. Father, Son, and Holy Spirit are said to share the same "substance," the same "essence"—the same "Godness"—with each other. They share divinity. They are an inseparable unity. They share an eternal indwelling with each other. They are fully, totally, completely, and ultimately "God." The three are one; the One is three. Father, Son, and Holy Spirit are one God in three persons.

The doctrine of the Trinity is hard to understand and explain. It is ultimately a mystery. For example, we recognize an important aspect of language about the Trinity. Though we speak of "Father" and "Son," we know that as God, God has no "gender." For some this has been a stumbling block because the use of "male" language connotes God as male, and further, for some, it elevates the "male as God." We know that this is not the intention of the language of the Trinity. God is "spirit" (John 4:24). The categories of "male" and "female" do not apply to God. We may think of the language of "Father" and "Son" as relational terms, indicating the identity of the "first person" of the Trinity in relation to the "second person" of the Trinity. But the problem of Trinitarian language is one of the indications of how difficult it is to speak of the Trinity and to try to understand it.

Yet in a real sense the Trinity is the starting point for all Christian theology. This is because theology means thought or talk about God. If we are doing Christian theology, we must be clear on what kind of God we are talking about—we must be clear on who God is. The answer of the Presbyterian tradition is the same answer we share with all Christians: We believe in one God in three persons. For us, the eternal God is related to us in these three persons. We do not worship, or discuss, or know any other "god." God as Trinity is the only source for our theology. This God is the one divine reality. God as Trinity is the way God relates to humanity and the God whom the church knows. It is this God who has reached out to provide salvation for the world. Throughout all that follows, in every other theological question with which we deal, we will be assuming that this is the God of whom we speak: God as Father, Son, and Holy Spirit.

Who Is God?

But who is this God whom we know as Father, Son, and Holy Spirit? God can be "defined" in a number of different ways. Throughout the Scriptures God is described as having many characteristics or attributes: God is love (1 John 4:8), righteous (Ps. 7:9, 11), merciful (Ex. 34:6), just (Isa. 30:18), to name just a few. One verse from the Psalms draws some of these characteristics together: "Gracious is the LORD, and righteous; our God is merciful" (Ps. 116:5).

Theologians have amplified these descriptions as they've tried to draw together what the Scripture teaches about who God is. Here is one portrayal of God from the Westminster Confession, the seventeenth-century Reformed confession. "There is," says the confession,

> but one only living and true God, who is infinite in being and perfection, a most pure spirit, invisible, without body, parts, or passions, immutable, immense, eternal, incomprehensible, almighty; most wise, most holy, most free, most absolute, working all things according to the counsel of his own immutable and most righteous will, for his own glory; most loving, gracious, merciful, long-suffering, abundant in goodness and truth, forgiving iniquity, transgression, and sin; the rewarder of them that diligently seek him; and withal most just and terrible in his judgments; hating all sin, and who will by no means clear the guilty. (*BC* 6.011)

That's a mouthful! This is one attempt to capture a description of God in all God's greatness and majesty.

What this description points us toward is two dimensions of God. These are what theologians call God's "transcendence" and God's "immanence." God is transcendent in that God is "over and beyond" the world and all creation. God is supreme in the universe. God is great, "high and lofty" (Isa. 6:1). God is, as the confession says, "immense," "eternal," "almighty." God is transcendent.

But God is also "immanent." This means that God is "near" to creation and near to us. God is personal. As the confession says, God is "most loving, gracious, merciful, long-suffering, abundant in goodness and truth, forgiving iniquity, transgression, and sin." God is involved in this world, as a personal God. God is near to us. The greatness and transcendence of God do not make God totally remote. God is a personal, loving God who enters into the life of creation and into each of our lives.

As Presbyterian Christians, we begin with the Trinity. We believe in one God, whom we know in three persons: Father, Son, and Holy Spirit. The works of each of the three persons is the work of one God. The one God works within the cosmos in three distinct ways: as Father, Son, and Holy Spirit.

Our first confession about God is usually that we believe in "God the Father Almighty, Maker of heaven and earth." These are the opening words of the Apostles' Creed. The core affirmations of this creed began to take shape very early in Christian history. The Bible associates the work of creation with God. We're familiar with the opening words of the Bible in the book of Genesis: "In the beginning when God created the heaven and the earth . . ." (Gen. 1:1). At other points in the Bible, the work of creation is also spoken of in relation to God the Son. For example, in John 1:3, in speaking about Jesus Christ as the eternal Logos, the text says that "all things came into being through him"—that is, through Jesus Christ. The apostle Paul, in Col. 1:16, says of Jesus Christ: "All things have been created through him and for him." This points us to the principle we just mentioned. The works of each of the members of the Trinity are the works of the whole Trinity. Typically, we consider the work of the Father to be in relation to creation; the work of the Son to be salvation or reconciliation; and the work of the Spirit to be to create new life. But God is one, and the work of one person of the Trinity is also the work of the whole Trinity.

The Trinity and Daily Life

The Trinity is one of the most difficult Christian doctrines to understand. Ultimately, we cannot "understand" it, since we are limited humans trying to fathom the transcendent God, who is over and beyond us. God is "God" and we are "humans." How God can exist as "one God in three persons" is a mystery that cannot be "explained" as much as "confessed" and believed as an expression of faith.

Yet, though the Trinity can seem very technical and abstract, it is crucial in Presbyterian theology for our understanding of God. All our talk in "theology"—the study of God—is based on who we believe God is as one God in three persons. But the Trinity is also a doctrine with very practical implications for daily life. Not only does the Trinity orient us toward what to believe about God, it also shapes us by giving directions for our belief and action every day.

For one thing, the Trinity means we can trust God. That is, what we know of God through the Scriptures as Father, Son, and Holy Spirit is consistent with the inner nature of the triune God. The way God is portrayed in Scripture and the way God acts in the world today are consistent with each other. We do not have to worry that we are being "fooled" and that the God who is revealed to us is different in nature than the God who exists eternally in a unity in three persons. This gives us confidence that we will not be led astray into views of God that are not consistent with who God really is. We have a trustworthy revelation of God.

Second, the Trinity is very practical for us in that it points us to the relational nature of our lives. One God in three Persons is a "relational" idea. The three persons of the Trinity relate to each other in divine love, in a mutual "indwelling" of divine love, that characterizes their divine life. Each member of the Trinity has a distinct identity in relationship to the other members. The "Son" is "Son" in relation to the Father and the Spirit; the "Spirit" is

To know God is to love others. The model of our love is the love that exists in the eternal Trinity among Father, Son, and Holy Spirit.

"Spirit" in relation to "Son" and "Father." What are the implications of this? Surely this means that just as love characterizes the eternal Trinity, so love should characterize our lives as well. If we say "God is love" (1 John 4:7–21) then we are to "love one another, because love is from God; everyone who loves is born of God and knows God" (1 John 4:7). To know God is to love others. The model of our love is the love that exists in the eternal Trinity among Father, Son, and Holy Spirit. We reflect that love as we live our lives in relationship with others, as God intends.

A third practical implication of the Trinity is that our lives are oriented to equality and justice. Love expresses itself in the drive to justice, peace, and equity among peoples. As the three persons of the Trinity are all equal in power and glory and share a mutual indwelling of love, so our human societies and human lives should mirror that same equality. The early church rejected all efforts to make the Trinity into a "hierarchical" belief—with one member "superior" or the "ruler" over the others (see the comments on "subordinationism" above). Instead, the church affirms that the three persons of the Trinity are all equally God. We recognize this same equality as persons among persons, seeking to image the divine community of the Trinity on a human level. Our lives corporately and personally should be directed toward treating others in ways consistent with the divine Godhead. This can lead us into concerns and actions to establish justice and peace within our societies and in the relationships we have with others in our homes and families and communities.

In these ways, our understandings of the Trinity can dramatically affect the ways we live. Our perception of one God in three persons can give us a trajectory for living that can move our lives in significant directions. When we ask, "Who is God?" and answer, "God is one God in three persons," our lives and thoughts can take us in unexpected directions.

Questions for Discussion

1. Why do Presbyterians believe in the Trinity?
2. Why is it important to understand that God is both "transcendent" and "immanent"?

3. Do you tend to think more often of one member of the Trinity than of the others? Why, or why not?
4. How do you envision the relationships among Father, Son, and Holy Spirit?
5. If the three members of the Trinity share an equality, what does that imply for relationships in the human community?

3

Creation

God is creator. God is the creator of "all things visible and invisible," of all things "seen and unseen." These phrases are from different versions of the Nicene Creed, a very old Christian affirmation, and are our basic confession about God. God is sovereign, we say, over all things. God created all things. God rules all things. All things have their origins with God.

Our world has its origin with God. This is something that all Christians confess as a very basic affirmation. God is the one who stands behind it all. Where Christians have sometimes disagreed, however, is when we go on to speculate about how the world was created by God, about the process of creation. We read of God's creation of the world in the first chapter of the first book in the Bible, the book of Genesis. The first verse of the Bible indicates that God "created the heavens and the earth," "in the beginning" (Gen. 1:1). The next verses go on to narrate God's creation of all else—including human beings. Some have taken the accounts that tell us about God as creator and have interpreted them in a straight-forward, literal fashion. They read the Genesis stories of creation as a historical narrative. This leads to beliefs about *how* God created the world and all that is in it: in six literal days, according to a certain order that is indicated in the biblical accounts.

But biblical scholars have helped us understand that those early chapters in Genesis need not be read in that literal way in order still to be true. Those chapters, as indeed the whole of the Bible, were written to tell us something of tremendous importance. They were written to affirm the reality of God and that God is the creator of all things. The Genesis accounts tell us this truth in structured stories. When we read these verses we need to realize this purpose. The purpose of the creation stories is not to tell us *how* God created; their purpose is to tell us *that* God created all things—"all things visible and invisible." The stories have a theological purpose.

This theological purpose is true regardless of the details of the story. We know, for example, that Jesus told parables (see Matt. 13). These also are stories that are to teach us theological truths. But it is not crucial for the theological truth of the parable that the events related in the parables ever actually, historically occurred. The truths of the parables transcend the questions about their historicity. In the same way, what is important to affirm, biblically, is the theological truth of the opening chapters of Genesis and, indeed, what is found in the rest of Scripture: that God is the creator of all things. Our world has its origins with God. The method or way in which God carried out the divine creative purposes in fashioning the universe and all within it is not the main point. The main point is to see and believe that behind all things, "seen and unseen," is the creative power of the divine creator, God.

> The purpose of the creation stories is not to tell us *how* God created; their purpose is to tell us *that* God created all things—"all things visible and invisible."

There are many implications of affirming that God is the creator of all. For one thing, this means that all the created order belongs to God. In the words of the psalmist: "The earth is the Lord's and all that is in it, the world, and those who live in it" (Ps. 24:1). Our natural environment belongs to God. The world as we know it existed long before humans came onto the scene. The natural world is God's world, since God is its creator. Humans are God's creatures, since ultimately our existence depends on God as well. We are born, given the breath of life, and live out our days. During this time we have a special responsibility to be good stewards, or caretakers, of the natural world. We are to use the world in accord with God's purposes—because the whole earth is the Lord's. We are the Lord's. God is the one who is Lord of all. Our whole attitudes about the environment, about how we use the earth's resources, about our lifestyles in relation to nature around us—all these relate theologically to the conviction that God is the creator of all things. What we do with God's creation is our responsibility. But what we do as Christians—as Presbyterian Christians—should emerge out of our theological certainty that God is the Lord of all, the creator of all.

A second affirmation of God as creator is that God has created us as well. As humans we have our origins with God. God created the world, and God created us. The biblical stories about creation indicate this clearly. Humans owe their origins to the breath of God, which in the Genesis story is breathed into the figures called Adam and Eve to make them become living beings (Gen. 2:7). Humans are the climax of God's creative activities and have their origins with God's creative actions. Again, the biblical accounts are not saying *how* God did this—how God made humans alive, as living beings. But the Bible affirms that God *is* the one who brought forth our existence and that we owe our origins to God's creative actions. We affirm that each new life, each baby, and each one of us is created by God. We know the biology about how life is created; we know the physical processes of conception, gestation, and birth—the so-called "facts of life." But we also know, as Christians, that the physical is not the only dimension. There is also the theological dimension. This is where we say that God created us. Our parents created us—in a sense. But in a bigger and even more important sense we affirm that we are created by the power and love of the living God.

A third implication of God as creator is to affirm that God is sovereign in creation. There are no other powers in the universe that can rival God's power. Our Christian tradition has affirmed that God created all things "out of nothing" (Lat. *ex nihilo*). That is, there are no other competing gods or lesser gods than the true God. There are no other gods with the same power to create as belongs to the true and living God of the Scriptures. As Christians, we believe that before the world was created there was nothing except God. There was no other "stuff" floating around—no "matter" or persons or power—just God. The one God whom we worship today is the same God who has existed eternally, and who created all things—visible and invisible—out of nothing. God's creative power and act brought all things into existence. Just how that happened, again, we do not learn from the Bible, and we should not turn to the Scriptures expecting to find out. The Bible tells us *that* God creates, not *how* God creates. But create God does!

Presbyterians have also recognized that God's sovereignty in creation means that God's divine will is the power and purpose behind the universe. There is no authority "higher" than the will of God. God's will stands behind the creation of all things.

An implication of this for human existence is that all creatures of God, who owe their existence to God's creative power, also owe their full lives to their creator as well. We who are God's creatures are created to obey God and to see God's will in all areas of our lives. The relationship between creator and creature is the most basic, most fundamental, of all relationships we can image. If this is so, then our whole orientations in life, our whole purposes and desires in life, should be to love, honor, and obey our creator. This is the message the Bible conveys. God's commands to Adam and Eve in the Garden of Eden in the Genesis story indicate that God has provided for the couple and that their response to God's gracious provisions for them is to obey God and live in the relationship God intends to have with them as creator and creature. God's sovereignty in creation relegates all other powers and all other "lords" to a secondary position. Humans belong to God. Ultimately it is the will and purposes of God that give structure and meaning to human life because God is our creator. If humans lose sight of this reality, we will lose our way in finding a purposeful and meaningful existence.

> . . . all creatures of God, who owe their existence to God's creative power, also owe their full lives to their creator as well.

Finally, our confession of God as creator assures us that our lives do have meaning and purpose. Our existence is rooted in the divine will. Our lives are anchored in the will of the one who has created the universe and all that is in it. God has created us and created all things for the divine purposes known only to God. The God who creates us, we will see, is also the God who loves us, redeems us, and calls us into lives of service. When we respond to our creator God in these ways, we find we are living life to the fullest. We are fulfilling the divine intention that created us. We are being all that we can be because our own purposes are joined with those of the One who has made us and given us the breath of life. The lives we live will find their true meaning and significance only if they are joined to the purposes of our creator. So to acknowledge God as creator and to find our true lives in the life God calls us toward is to live life as God intended. This is the highest fulfillment and the truest joy we can know.

So this is our Christian confession. God created and, as the Bible says, God looked upon the creation and it was "very good" (Gen. 1:31). This is our affirmation as well. God has created all things, including us; and what God has created is, indeed, "very good"!

Questions for Discussion

1. Why is it important to affirm that God is the creator of "all things visible and invisible"?
2. What difference does it make whether or not we interpret the early chapters of Genesis "literally"?
3. Why is it important to affirm that all that God creates is "good"?
4. Do you think Presbyterians put enough emphasis on God as the creator? Why, or why not?
5. What are some implications of the doctrine of creation for everyday life?

4

Providence

*T*he sovereign God who creates is also the God who guides. This is the Christian doctrine of providence. In a general way, all Christians affirm that God guides the universe, the world, and human history. Presbyterian theologians have developed this view in more detail than have many others. What is affirmed here is the breathtaking contention that no part of God's created work is excluded from God's divine direction and care.

Parts of Providence

Reformed theology has typically seen the doctrine of providence as having three parts: God preserves the creation; God cooperates with all created beings; and God guides all things toward the accomplishment of God's ultimate purposes. These are three ways of describing God's overarching involvement in the created order and with the creatures whom God creates.

Preservation. God preserves the creation. If God had simply brought all things into being by an act of creation and then stopped, what would have happened? The answer is that everything that was created would instantly cease to exist. If there were no divine power to uphold what is created, then the created order would have collapsed into nothingness.

But God preserves the creation by sustaining it. God continues to exercise a divine energy to see that the creation is maintained, upheld, and preserved. Order prevails and life can continue to develop because there is the supporting power of God to enable the world to continue to exist. We believe the world will not collapse into nothingness, because God's almighty power continues to uphold. Our lives will not simply collapse, because that same power of God is there to sustain us. The psalmist put it very simply: "I lie down and sleep; I wake again, for the LORD sustains me" (Ps. 3:5). This is a most comforting thought!

Cooperation. God also cooperates with all created beings. God's power cooperates with all lesser powers in the universe. Our human powers cooperate with God's divine powers to maintain and sustain life. God works with us and in us and through us to do what God wants done in this world. In one sense, we do not act solely by ourselves: because God's power is at work within us. But we do act—we *really* act—because we function by using the powers that God has created within us to use. We act freely—according to our own wills. We make decisions.

> We act freely—according to our own wills. Yet, at the same time, we can believe that our will is cooperating with God's will to carry out God's ultimate divine purposes.

We listen to our "hearts" and our "heads," and our "hands" do their bidding. So we carry out our desires. Yet, at the same time, we can believe that our will is cooperating with God's will to carry out God's ultimate divine purposes. God works in us and through us to accomplish the divine will in conjunction with our wills. This wisdom is expressed in the book of Proverbs, where the writer maintains that "the human mind plans the way, but the LORD directs the steps" (Prov. 16:9).

How all this works—well, it's a mystery. The philosophers and theologians have debated it for centuries. How can the divine and the human work together? For many people, no satisfying intellectual or rational explanation can be found. But as Christians we confess it. One of the amazing "ways of God" is to enable this "both/and" condition to occur. God is sovereign; humans are free to make choices. The Scriptures testify to both aspects. As Presbyterian Christians, we affirm it. God works through human beings, through our desires and choices, as the "means" of accomplishing

God's divine purposes for the world and in human life. Part of God's providence is to cooperate with us and with all creatures in the universe.

Guidance. A third dimension of God's providence is God's guidance. The whole universe was created by God, it is sustained by God, and God is at work within it. God is at work within the universe, within our world in human history—and in our own individual lives—to guide all things to God's final ends or purposes.

God directs, steers, and carries out the divine will to guide all things to their ultimate ends or purposes. God is at work in nature. God is at work in history. Not only is the eye of God "over" history, but the hand of God is also "in" history. The psalmist used the language of authority in the ancient world to express this: "The LORD has established his throne in the heavens, and his kingdom rules over all" (Ps. 103:19).

> God is at work in each individual human life to lead and guide that life according to the divine will. This is a "lively" sense of providence.

God is at work in each individual human life to lead and guide that life according to the divine will. This is a "lively" sense of providence. This conviction has been especially important for Presbyterian Christians. It has fueled Presbyterians to be particularly active in society, because we believe that God is at work with us in history to accomplish the divine will and purposes. The sense of God leading our lives has been of great personal importance to Presbyterian people as well. The Puritans in the seventeenth century, as acts of Christian devotion, used to keep an account in their diaries of "God's providences." They saw the hand of God at work in their lives directing them and being concerned with even the smallest details of their existence, just as Jesus had indicated (see Matt. 10:29–30).

Comforts and Challenges

It is ultimately this conviction that the God who preserves, cooperates, and guides is the God of our Lord Jesus Christ that enables us to trust in the providence of God. Any religious system, for example, may believe in a power that created the world, that sustains the world, is operative in the world, and guides the world to an appointed end. But the Christian doctrine of providence is unique because it sees the God who sustains, cooperates, and guides as the same God who is the "Father of our Lord Jesus Christ" (2 Cor. 1:3). Indeed, we might say, the "eternal Father of our Lord Jesus Christ," since we are speaking here of the eternal Trinity of Father, Son, and Holy Spirit.

Christian theologians have also sought to distinguish the Christian view of providence from the Stoic belief in fate. The Stoics were ancient philosophers who believed that the universe was unfolding according to the "laws of nature," the blind fate that was built into the character of the universe itself. So things happened inevitably—there was nothing humans could do about events: "Whatever will be, will be."

Yet the Presbyterian perception of providence is that the one who sustains, cooperates, and guides the world is also the One who has created the world and who shares the life of the eternal Trinity with the Holy Spirit and as the Father of our Lord Jesus Christ. This is the God who is revealed in the Scriptures and the God who is the God who loves the world in Jesus Christ (John 3:16). So it is not "blind fate" that shapes destinies. The Christian looks instead to the benevolent God who has provided for the world by continuing to sustain it, cooperating with those who are created, and guiding the world toward the ultimate end of history—the reign of God, when "the kingdom of the world has become the kingdom of our Lord and of his Messiah, and he will reign forever and ever" (Rev. 11:15).

To recognize that the God of providence is the same God who is revealed in Jesus Christ is an important dimension when we see that this understanding of God's providence is both a comfort and a challenge for Presbyterians.

Comforts. John Calvin devoted a chapter in his *Institutes* to providence (*Institutes* 1.17). He was concerned that Christian believers be able to apply this doctrine to their greatest benefit. God's benevolence and kindness in providence, in Calvin's view, sets us free "from every care." The result is that "gratitude of mind for the favorable outcome of things, patience in adversity, and also incredible freedom from worry about the future all necessarily follow upon this knowledge" (*Institutes* 1.17.7). In both the good and bad times in human life, we can trust God's providence to sustain us, work with us, and guide us. Calvin's language is similar to the answer to the question: "How does the knowledge of God's creation and providence help us?" found in the Heidelberg Catechism (1563), one of the most influential catechisms of the Reformed faith. The answer is: "We can be patient when things go against us, thankful when things go well, and for the future we can have good confidence in our faithful God and Father that nothing in creation will separate us from his love. For all creatures are so completely in God's hand that without his will they can neither move nor be moved." (*BC* 4.028). The strong assurance that we can trust "our faithful God and Father for the future" sustains us in the midst of the difficulties we face in life as well as giving us the confidence of the "children of God" (Rom. 8:21) to accept God's blessings with gratitude.

Challenges. Along with comforts come challenges. The doctrine of God's providence also raises in our minds some disturbing questions: If God is leading and guiding the world and our lives, why is there evil in the world? Why do people suffer if God is a God of love and mercy and if God's purposes are being carried out in the world? These issues are part of all thoughtful Christian reflection at some point. They can pose challenges to our belief in God's providence.

Evil is a reality. Christian theology always affirms this. Evil is that which opposes God and the divine will. Why there is evil in the world, we do not know. The origin of evil is a mystery. We do not believe God "sends" evil or "wills" evil, since that would be contrary to God's essential character of love (1 John 4:8, 16) and mercy (Ps. 116:5). What we do believe is that God can use the evil, which is part of our world and intrudes on our lives, for good. God's providential purposes can be served as God works within us and through us to turn evil, suffering, and all that works against God's will into God's ultimate, sovereign purposes. We see this, for example, in the experience of Joseph in the Old Testament. After he was sold by his brothers into slavery in Egypt, Joseph eventually came to the place where, as a person in power, he confronted his brothers, who had come to him for help. As he considered the ways in which his brothers had treated him, and then what had happened to him since, Joseph was able to affirm, "Even though you intended to do harm to me, God intended it for good, in order to preserve a numerous people, as he is doing today" (Gen. 50:20). God was able to work with the evil intended by Joseph's brothers and turn it into an ultimate good.

We can never simply dismiss evil as being of no consequence, or think that suffering in this life is unreal or something from which we can be exempt. But in the midst of evil—even the evils of terrorism, war, famine, disaster, and disease—the promise of the Scriptures is that God is with us and that through God's continuing, providential presence, God can bring good out of evil and suffering. God has the power and the will to do so. This was the faith that propelled the apostle Paul to affirm: "We know that all things work together for good for those who love God, who are called according to his purpose" (Rom. 8:28). God's will ultimately triumphs over evil and suffering. We have this assurance in Jesus Christ himself, who in his resurrection made this triumph sure (Eph. 1:20–23; Col. 1:15–20). The challenges to belief in God's providence are real. But our faith is grounded in God's purposes, which will triumph at the last (1 Cor. 15:57; 1 John 5:4). Presbyterians believe in providence and affirm with John Calvin that "ignorance of providence is the ultimate of all miseries; the highest blessedness lies in the knowledge of it" (*Institutes* 1.17.11).

Uses

Preservation, cooperation, and guidance. The doctrine of providence is both an extremely comforting as well as an extremely challenging doctrine. It assures us that our world and our lives are held secure in God's hand. God preserves creation and our own human existence. It presents challenges to us when we face evil and suffering. Yet it also challenges us in all times to cooperate with God's purposes in this world, to live according to God's divine will, and to seek that will for our lives above all else. It is God's will that is for our own best good. Some days it is hard to believe that! But belief in the providence of God helps us recognize that God is guiding our lives, directing our circumstances, relationships, and course in life. This gives us the blessed assurance that God is at work within us and among us to accomplish the divine will and plan. This can give us the greatest joys and comforts in our lives.

Questions for Discussion

1. Do you often think of providence as part of your Christian experience? Why, or why not?
2. Why is it important to recognize all the "Parts of Providence" (preservation, cooperation, and guidance)?
3. How do you understand the relation between God's providence and human choices?
4. What examples of God's providence do you recognize in your own life?
5. What are the comforts and the challenges of providence for your own Christian life?

PART II

The Christ Who Saves People like Us

Humanity

At some time or other, most thoughtful persons ask themselves this question: Who am I? This is the question of self-identity. It is one of the most basic issues with which we have to deal as human beings. We recognize ourselves as humans—as part of the human race, along with countless millions of people throughout the world. We know we are part of the human family. But we ask ourselves: What does this mean? What does it mean to be part of the human race, to be a human being? What does it mean to be the person I am, the unique individual that I see in the mirror each day? Who am I? This is a basic issue because it directly affects us. We need to know and understand what our nature is, who we are, and even more broadly: Why are we here? What is the purpose of my life?

As Christians, the question is important as well. Our understanding of the Christian faith supposes certain theological truths about human beings. In our Presbyterian tradition, certain emphases have been prominent, and certain theological understandings about human beings have been important. Presbyterians share some common views with all Christian theologians, as well as some particular perspectives that we believe are consistent with the teachings of the Scriptures.

Created as Whole Persons

The biblical stories in the book of Genesis make it clear that God is the creator of all things and that God is the creator of human beings. The two creation accounts in Genesis that deal with the creation of humans (Gen. 1:26–31; Gen. 2:7–25) both attribute the creation of human beings to the breath (Gen. 2:7) and power of God (Gen. 1:27). God's creative power in bringing us as humans into existence is recognized throughout the Scriptures (Pss. 8; 100:3; Mal. 2:10).

Biblical accounts use certain terms to describe the makeup of humans: body, soul, and spirit are most common. But we also encounter other terms such as flesh, heart, mind, and conscience. Often these words are used as a kind of shorthand to refer to the whole person. The Bible certainly views humans as both "bodily" and "spiritual" beings, in the sense that while we are physical beings, we are much more. We have dimensions of ourselves ("personalities," we would say) that are capable of expressing emotions, choosing, acting, and relating to other persons. How we choose to use these aspects of ourselves is of great concern in the Bible and to the God who has created us.

> We are created as whole persons, and God is concerned about the totality of our existence.

Humans are complex persons. We know this now, in our own experience, in ways far different from and beyond what biblical writers envisioned. But biblical perspectives on who we are still speak powerfully to us: We are created as whole persons, and God is concerned about the totality of our existence. This concern is clearly expressed in the summary of the Hebrew law that Jesus expressed, echoing the great commandment that God gave to Israel (Deut. 6:5). Jesus said that the way to true or "eternal" life—the purpose of our creation by God— is to "love the Lord your God with all your heart, and with all your soul, and with all your strength, and with all your mind; and your neighbor as yourself" (Luke 10:27). God wants us to be devoted in our love for God—with our whole selves. The whole person is created by God, and the whole person "belongs" to God, and we are expected to love God with all that is within us and constitutes us. God wants a comprehensive commitment of the whole person.

God is concerned with our lives in their totality. So God is concerned with our lives in all their fullness. There are no arenas of our existence in which God has no interest. The Old Testament prophets cry out for justice and for God's righteousness to take shape in their society, a justice and righteousness that relate to people's everyday lives (Isa. 28:17; 61:8; Amos 5:15, 24; Mic. 6:8). God is concerned with hunger (Ps. 107:9; cf. Matt. 25:35) and even sleep (Pss. 3:5; 4:8)! And, of course, God is concerned with other human attitudes, actions, emotions, thoughts, and speech (Prov. 8:13; Pss. 34:14; 139:23; Prov. 12:6).

All this points us to recognizing that as humans we are created by God as whole persons, persons about whom God cares in our entirety. This is a blessing of being human: there is no problem, no issue, no difficulty in any area of our lives about which God does not care. Our health, family, communities, nations—all are of concern to God. Our attitudes, minds, and hearts—these are of concern to God as well. If we are to mirror God in our daily lives, we will have similar concerns for the lives of others. We will care for them in a comprehensive manner. We will not think that we are to deal only with "spiritual issues." We will seek the good of others in every dimension of their existence. Since we are created as whole persons, we will care for others in the fullness of their lives, just as God cares for us in every dimension of who we are as humans.

> Since we are created as whole persons, we will care for others in the fullness of their lives, just as God cares for us in every dimension of who we are as humans.

Image of God

Our creation by God is marked also by a further dimension. A most basic conviction we share with all Christians is that as humans we are created by God in the image of God. The creation stories in the book of Genesis describe, in differing ways, that God created human beings. Genesis 1:26–27 indicates that humans are created in the "image" and "likeness" of God. Theologically, this points us to a very significant fact. As Christians we believe we cannot understand who we are as human beings without realizing that we are creatures of God. We are created by God, and we are created in God's image. This means that our human existence is inextricably connected to God. We live, as human beings, in some kind of relationship with our creator. What that relationship is—that is the question. But related we are. We encounter many different ways of looking at humans. There are the approaches of the social sciences, such as psychology or sociology or anthropology. These views look at different dimensions of human beings—their psyches, their social relationships, their cultural customs. Yet these disciplines cannot show us the whole picture of who humans are. None of them conveys the fullness of who we are. Nor can any of these disciplines give us what we as Christians regard as the most important dimension to humanity: the fact that as humans we are related to God. Because God is our creator and because we are created in the image of God, we are related to God. This is, fundamentally, the most important fact of our existence. We cannot think of ourselves—or of humanity as a whole—apart from this basic conviction: We are created by God and created in the image of God. If so, then all our "anthropology" must be "theological anthropology." That is, from the perspectives of Christian faith, we must view ourselves in the light of our fundamental relationship with our creator. Social sciences give us important and valuable insights into dimensions of human existence. But our most basic conviction is theological.

We are created in the "image of God." This phrase, while important in Christian theology, is a phrase that has been interpreted in a number of ways. What does it mean to say that we are created in God's image? In what ways are we like God? In what ways are we different from God?

One way of understanding humans as created in the divine image is to consider humans to be divine "image bearers." In other words, as created by God, humans are to represent God or to bear God's image to others. We are to "image God" to other people. In ancient times, an emperor who ruled over a kingdom could not be present at every place or in every land under the emperor's control. So the emperor would have statues erected in various places. These statues of the emperor would remind everyone who saw them that the emperor was the ruler. They bore the emperor's "image" and thus represented the emperor throughout the whole empire.

In the same way, humans created in the image of God are to "represent" God—the ruler—in every place and in every relationship. When people encounter us, they should see God living in us. We are God's representatives through-

> . . . as created by God, humans are to represent God or to bear God's image to others. We are to "image God" to other people.

out the whole world. We were created in the image of God in order to be God's eyes and ears and hands throughout the whole earth. We are created in the image of God in order to "image" God to other people.

On the other hand, if we are created in the divine image, then we should recognize that image in every other person. We recognize people at the most basic level—not on the basis of their gender, or their race, or their economic situation, but as fellow creatures, created in the image of God. We are united with all others in this world by this most basic of all bonds. We are united on the basis of our common humanity as creatures created in the image of God. This is our most central conviction about who we are as humans, and who others are: We are all creatures of God who bear the divine image and likeness. Of course, we encounter differentiations. Humans are unique, distinctive. Each of us is different. Yet, we are also all the same. Our "sameness" is that we are all divine image bearers.

What is the significance of being created in the image of God? Theologically, our creation in the image of God means that as humans we have a special standing before God. Humans stand apart from all other aspects of God's creation in that we have received the breath of life from God, and have been created for a special relationship with God that no other of the created creatures has. Humans are to be stewards of the earth, to manage the resources of the earth, on God's behalf. Humans are God's representatives on earth, and are to reflect to the created order the nature of God, the creator of all things. In this sense, humans join as partners with God. We use the freedom God gives us to be united with God's purposes for this world.

Theologically, our creation in the image of God also means that as humans we are to love God as our creator. We are to obey God, because God is our Lord, our Sovereign, our Creator. We are to love and live in the special relationship God intends. We are to obey God and live according to God's will and purposes for our lives. We, as humans created in the image of God, depend on God for all things. We look to God for guidance in our lives. We reflect God's image to others. Being created in the image of God is the most basic thing that can be said about us. We love God, we obey God, we depend on God—because God has created us in this relationship. We are created in the image of God.

But even more, to be created in the image of God is to realize that humans are created for community. We are created for fellowship with God and for community with one another. One of our Presbyterian confessions, a Brief Statement of Faith (1991), puts it this way:

> In sovereign love God created the world good
> and makes everyone equally in God's image,
>   male and female, of every race and people,
> to live as one community. (BC 10.3)

God creates a human family. God does not create one person and then call it quits. The stories in the book of Genesis show how God intends and desires for humans to be in relation with one another. Just as the doctrine of the Trinity points us to the divine interrelationships, so the doctrine of the image of God (Lat. *imago Dei*) points us to the divine intention that humans live in communal relationships with one another. The love God showed in creating humans is to be shared by humans with one another. All through their human history this shared love is the divine intention for human beings.

Questions for Discussion

1. Do you spend much time wondering: Who am I? Why, or why not?
2. Why is it important to have a "theological view" of humanity?

3. What difference does it make in your views of others to see them as created in the "image of God"?
4. What are some practical implications of saying that we are created in the "image of God"?
5. In what ways do you "represent God" in your daily life? How can the church do this?

6

Sin

While humans are created in the image of God, the Bible and Presbyterian theology in particular recognize that the relationship of love that humans were created to share with God and with each other has been broken. This disruption is called "sin." All through the Scriptures, the Bible indicates that humans turn out not to be the people they were created by God to be. The human community is upset; the fellowship of humans with their creator is disrupted. Sin is a fact of human existence that radically alters the relationship humans were created to have with God and with each other. As human beings, we are sinners.

This is the paradox of human existence. Humans are created as the crown of God's creation—as the creatures who enjoy a special standing before God and a special relationship with God. But now, humans have slipped into another condition. That condition is a relationship with God that is not marked by love, as God intends, but by selfishness, pride, and the refusal to recognize that God is the Lord, the creator and the Lord who orders all human life. Human sin is an expression of the evil within the universe. Evil is that which stands counter to or against God and God's will. As humans who are sinners, we share in this evil.

> Human sin is an expression of the evil within the universe.

Presbyterians have strongly emphasized the doctrine of sin. This is because we believe that the Bible takes sin very seriously.

In fact, one might say that sin is the most serious fact of human existence.

Presbyterian theology regards humans as sinners by nature. To say that we are sinners by nature means that if left on our own, we will always act according to who we are, or according to our nature. Our nature is to be sinners. We sin. We do what is wrong in the sight of God. Left to ourselves, we will always be sinners. We will always choose to go our own ways instead of going God's ways. We will always seek our own good rather than God's will or the good of others. Our outward actions will always be expressions of our inward nature. And our nature is to be disobedient to God's will and to seek to do our own will instead.

Images of Sin

We are familiar with the number of ways the Bible portrays sin. Sin is iniquity, transgression, revolt, or missing the mark: sin is lawlessness, ignorance, pride, an offense against God. All of these are biblical images. They point to the basic message about sin: sin is what we do that is against God. Sin is what we do that is against God's purposes. Sins are the acts we do. When we oppose God and God's will, we sin. This sin can take any number of forms in our lives. One of the most basic forms is what the Bible calls idolatry. Idolatry is our basic tendency to worship or put an ultimate value on things that are other than God. When we in effect worship anything or person other than the living God, we are guilty of idolatry. Idolatry is worshiping that which is less than God, that in which we choose to invest our efforts and values. So sin is what we do.

We sin both as individuals and corporately, as collective groups of people in society. Sin in society takes many insidious forms: violence, racism, sexism, oppression. The sad history of human aggression as nations fight against nations, as violence flares, and as people are deprived of human dignity and human rights, and the destruction of our environment are painful reminders of some of the ways sin is corporately expressed. If we need proof that the human race as a whole is sinful, we need only look at the news—any day! Structures of society, institutions, and entrenched powers are arenas sin inhabits. Despite outward appearances of propriety and responsibility, the power of sin is resident throughout even our best-intentioned organizations. What we do corporately reflects who we are personally. What we do is sinful when our corporate actions violate God's will and purposes.

Yet Presbyterian theology has also stressed that sin is not only actions. Sin is also a condition or a state of being. This is actually the cause for our sinful actions. We do sinful things because by nature we are sinful people. Our natural condition, as human beings, is the condition of sinfulness. All of us share in this situation. We are all sinners in God's sight. As the apostle Paul put it, "All have sinned and fall short of the glory of God" (Rom. 3:23). Left to ourselves, we will always choose to do sinful things. Why? We do sinful things because our condition or nature as people is sinful.

Original Sin

This is a pretty bleak picture, isn't it? We are sinners, we believe; and even more we are sinners by nature—it is our natural condition before God. Reformed theology has seen our sinfulness as emerging from what theologians call "original sin." "Original sin" refers to the conviction that all of us—the human race—are sinful in our origins. We are part of one race of people—a race of people who have chosen always to go our own ways instead of God's ways; who have sinned in the very essence of our beings. Traditionally, original sin has been linked with the biblical story of Adam and Eve in the book of Genesis. We remember in Genesis 3 the story of Adam and Eve's having eaten the forbidden fruit after being tempted by Satan. They ate—and then their fellowship with God was broken. It was broken because they did what God had told them not to do. They had disobeyed God, and then they suffered the consequences. They were expelled from the Garden of Eden, and they lost the perfect relationship with God that they had enjoyed until that point. Regardless of how you interpret the Adam and Eve story—either literally or symbolically—the theological truth remains. Humanity has turned away from God, disobeyed

God, rebelled against God, fractured the human/divine relationship. We find ourselves cut off, or separated from God.

Theologians have discussed how an action from the ancient past—whenever it may have occurred—can be transmitted to those who are born millennia later. Most commonly, in the Presbyterian tradition, there is the view that we are sinners by nature because our first ancestor—whoever that was—sinned, and in that sin represented us. We are in human solidarity, one with the other, from today back to the very origins of the race. In that solidarity, what one does affects all others. In our origins as a race of human beings, sin entered into our experience, and that sin is still present with us today. Since it is present with us today, we are all sinners by nature. We act in accord with who we are. And we are sinners. Sin is our natural condition. It is our nature. Left on our own, we reject God, turn our backs on God's will and God's ways for our lives. We would rather do things "our way" than see God's purposes for us. It is this rebellion, this lawlessness, this alienation from God that is the condition of sin in which we find ourselves.

> Sin is our natural condition. It is our nature. Left on our own, we reject God, turn our backs on God's will and God's ways for our lives.

The results of our natural condition as sinners are dramatic. Reformed theology has seen sin as radically affecting the whole human person. Sometimes this is called "total depravity." That does not mean that humans are so absolutely evil that they are "depraved," in the sense of being thoroughly and completely filled with evilness. It means instead that our sinfulness affects the totality of our existence. There are no areas or arenas in our human experience that are exempt from the effect of sin.

For one thing, our minds are affected. We do not use our reasoning powers to try to ascertain the mind and will of God for our lives. Instead, we use our intellects to justify our actions and to convince ourselves that living according to our own desires instead of God's desires is not so bad. Also, our relationships are affected. We use our personalities to advance ourselves, looking out always for our own best interests instead of the interests of others, seeking first our own good and not the good of other persons. Our human community, for which God created us and made us in the divine image — that community is fractured by sin.

Then, too, our wills are affected and corrupted by sin. This is a key theological point about which there have been many theological controversies. How much power to will the good does the sinful human will possess? Can humans, merely by "wanting to," do good, do God's will? Or is the will so affected by sin that it will always incline to the path of evil and selfishness? Is the sinful human will capable of responding to God's Word or God's grace? In these discussions, the Reformed view has always been on the side of recognizing the complete bondage of the human will to the power of sin. Left to ourselves, our own wills will never incline to accept God's Word or God's grace, because we are so totally and thoroughly in the grip of the power of sin. In this sense, we have no "free will." As Heinrich Bullinger wrote in the Second Helvetic Confession, "in regard to goodness and virtue," our human reason "does not judge rightly of itself concerning divine things." For humans who are "not yet regenerate" have "no free will for good, no strength to perform what is good" (*BC* 5.045, citing John 8:34 and Rom. 8:7). Sin inclines us toward ourselves instead of toward God — as our creator and Lord and as the one to whom we owe allegiance and obedience. We have turned away from God's love in the interest of loving ourselves; we have "missed the mark" — we have failed to be the people God wants and calls us to be.

Results of Sin

The result is that as humans we are people separated from God. We fail to live up to God's laws or to the kinds of lives God wants us to live. Our situation is that, by ourselves, we cannot do anything about it. We cannot do anything to change or alter ourselves — because we really don't want to do so. We are sinners. As sinners, we act in accordance with our natures, and those natures are natures that are set against God and against God's will for our lives. We sin by nature and by our choices. Our choices are an expression of our nature.

So our choices will be sinful. We are unable to change our natures by ourselves. These are the radical effects of sin, according to the Reformed tradition. We possess a sinful nature that we are totally unable to change by ourselves.

This is our state of sin, our total inability to lift ourselves up by our own bootstraps or to save ourselves from this condition. We cannot reestablish fellowship with God on our own. We cannot miraculously change ourselves, suddenly to become "saints" instead of sinners. We need, in other words, some power or someone who can do for us what we cannot do for ourselves. In short, we need a savior. We need a savior who can change our situations. We need a savior who can reestablish the relationship God desires to have with us as humans. We need someone who can also deal with the fact that our sin produces guilt within us. We stand guilty before God for all that we are and all that we have done. We need someone who can make our lives new. And, ultimately, we need someone who can save us from the death that our sin produces. We die, according to the Bible, because we are sinners. "The wages of sin is death," says the apostle Paul (Rom. 6:23). We need someone who can come to us in our sinfulness and do for us what we cannot do for ourselves—in short, save us.

> We possess a sinful nature that we are totally unable to change by ourselves. This is our state of sin.

Questions for Discussion

1. What evidence do you see that sin affects all areas of human life?
2. In what ways does the sin of "idolatry" express itself today?
3. What are the results of our "wills" being affected so strongly by sin?
4. Do you think Presbyterians emphasize sin enough today? Why, or why not?
5. What effects of sin do you see in society? in the church? in your life?

7

Christology

*I*n the midst of all this "bad news" about the human condition, the Christian faith, and also Presbyterian theology, proclaims "good news." The good news is that God has looked upon our situation and has acted on our behalf. God has come to us. God has come to us in Jesus Christ, God's eternal Son, to do for us what we could never do for ourselves—to save us. This is the "good news," or the gospel. It is the story of salvation. It is the greatest news the world can ever hear. It is the best message humans can ever experience. It is the message that can make all life new—both now and forever. God has come to this world and has lived among us (John 1:14). This has happened in Jesus Christ.

We call this the doctrine of the incarnation. The incarnation means "God has become flesh" or God has become a person. God has entered into the arena of our human experience and has become one of us. God is with us. The eternal God has become a human person. This is the meaning of the great text in the Gospel of John: "The Word became flesh and lived among us" (1:14). The second person of the Trinity, the eternal Son of God, has become a human being, has entered into the human condition and become a person just like us. He has identified with us, he has shared our sorrows, our joys, and our emotions. In Jesus Christ, God has taken on the human condition in all ways.

In all ways, that is, except one. Jesus Christ has become totally like us as human beings except that he did not sin. Jesus Christ is the one human being who remained totally faithful to God, in all things and in all ways. Jesus Christ was sinless. He is the only person about whom that can be said. He remained sinless because he was divine. But he was also human, and in his humanity he shares our lives as well. Jesus was tempted—tempted as we are—yet he did not give in to sin (Heb. 4:15). He maintained a fidelity to God that we ourselves cannot imitate successfully. But we can look to Jesus Christ who, as one of us, sought the will of God in every situation. Jesus was sinless.

Truly Divine and Truly Human

Presbyterian theology has always maintained that it is crucial for our faith that Jesus Christ—the Son of God—be both truly divine and truly human. In his humanity, Jesus did not lose his divinity. He was the second person of the Trinity. But in the incarnation he "emptied himself" as the letter to the Philippians says, "emptied himself" and "humbled himself," taking the form of a servant or a slave (Phil. 2:7–8). Jesus was divine and human at the same time. In the Gospels we read of his miracles—those events that seem to be possible only if God was involved—healing the sick, casting out demons, raising the dead. We see Jesus' miracles and we know he is divine. At the same time, we see Jesus' great humanity—his care and love, his human emotion. Remember how he wept when his friend Lazarus died (John 11:35)?

> Both Jesus' divinity and his humanity shine forth clearly in the biblical accounts. Both are significant.

Both Jesus' divinity and his humanity shine forth clearly in the biblical accounts. Both are significant.

We have said it is crucial for our faith that Jesus be both truly God and truly human. Jesus must be "truly God" in order to do for us what we cannot do for ourselves: save us. He must be truly God so that he has the power to be our Savior. If he were any less than "truly God," he would be no greater than any other human—no greater a figure than any of the heroes of humanity that we might look up to in admiration. Jesus must be "truly human" in order to be identified completely with humanity. If he were not "truly human," how could we believe that he was saving people like us? He would not be truly one of us, knowing us through and through, being tempted as we are—if he were not "truly human," he would not be able to reach us at the point of our greatest need, our sinfulness. This is what theologians refer to as the "two natures of Christ." Jesus Christ was truly God and truly human. He had a divine nature and a human nature. The two natures were united in one person ("hypostatic union"). Jesus did not have two personalities. He was not "half God" and "half human." He did not act "divine" half the time—on Mondays, Wednesdays, and Fridays—and "human" the rest of the week! Jesus was thoroughly God and thoroughly human. Fully God and fully human. Both natures are necessary if Jesus is to be who we proclaim him to be. He is the eternal Word of God who lived among us; he is "Emmanuel," which means "God with us." He is our great high priest, who was tempted as we are—yet without sinning (Heb. 2:17–18; 4:15).

So the good news of the Christian gospel is that God has looked upon us sinners—people who are separated from God, who are living according to our own agendas, falling short of the lives God wants us to have. God looks upon the likes of us and sends Jesus Christ into our world as truly God and as a truly human person. By coming into our world, Jesus acts to save us. By becoming one of us in Jesus Christ, God is not only "with us," but also "for us." God acts to save us by doing for us what we, in our sinfulness, cannot do for ourselves. Jesus acts to bring us salvation and to restore our relationship with God. This is our great need: to live in the loving, trustful relationship of faith that God desires. Our great need is to have our sins forgiven—the things we do that are contrary to God's will. Our great need is to have a new nature given to us—no longer a "sinful" nature, but now a nature that is able to love God in return and to live in ways that are in accord with God's will and purposes, because we want to do so. We need a new mind, a new heart, and a new will. We need, in other words, to be a "new creation." The astonishing news is that, in Jesus Christ, this new creation for us and for all humanity is possible (2 Cor. 5:17–19).

Atonement

Jesus has come to us as "truly God and truly human," and Jesus has died for us. This is the central focus of Christian faith: that God has come into this world in Jesus Christ, and that by his death on the cross Jesus has opened up for us a whole new possibility for living. This is why the central symbol of Christianity is the cross. On the cross on that Friday afternoon when Jesus died, an event occurred that has forever changed the reality of humanity. Jesus' death on the cross has brought about a new relationship between God and the world created by God but fallen into sin.

Forgiveness has occurred, and reconciliation is accomplished. Through the death of Jesus Christ, humans and God have been brought together again in the relationship intended in creation. This is a relationship of trust, love, and obedience instead of the sin that leads humans to be self-centered, afraid to trust, bound up only in their own concerns. Forgiveness brings pardon and mercy. Forgiveness is the establishment of a new status, or standing, in the relationship between God and sinners. Forgiveness means that the past is over and gone, that a "new creation" has occurred, and that a new life has become a reality (2 Cor. 5:17–21).

In the history of Christian theology, there have been a number of explanations of how the death of Christ leads to the forgiveness of our sins and our redemption, or reconciliation with God. The death of Christ is called, theologically, the doctrine of the atonement. Atonement means God and humans "at one," or reconciled with each other.

Images of Sin and Salvation

In the Bible we find a number of different images to describe the sinful conditions of humankind in relation to God. These images are taken from different realms of human experience. The images present a picture of the sinful conditions in which humans find themselves. There are images for the ways in which Jesus Christ has overcome these conditions. These images speak to us differently. They speak to our various conditions or stages of life. Where we experience need in terms of our sin, the image of Jesus' death on the cross meets us where we are and provides the answer to our deepest needs.

Forgiveness. In the personal realm, the Bible shows people as alienated from God. The human community God desires, of people with each other, is broken by sin—people looking out for themselves instead of for each other. We seek only our own agendas for our lives, adopt only our own priorities. But even more, people are alienated from God. This is separation and isolation. Sin drives a wedge in the relationship of love God seeks with God's creatures. So we are estranged, alienated, cut off from our loving creator. This is the sinful human condition. But the Bible also shows that Jesus Christ, in his death on the cross, has "bridged the gap" between God and humans. God has acted as a loving parent, Jesus has come as a mediator of love, and through his death on the cross Jesus has overcome this alienation and brought about reconciliation. In the cross, God has reached out in love to overcome our isolation and alienation. God has reached out in loving forgiveness to overcome the past and to create a new relationship of love and trust. The two sides that were cut off have now been made one; God and humans are "at one" through the death of God's Son. Now the love of God for humanity is shown. The price of this love is fully clear. God was willing to go to the point of death in order to bring humans into a reconciled relationship. In Jesus, this love is dramatically demonstrated. That is one meaning of the death of Christ, or the atonement. We can become children of God, children of our divine Parent in heaven, through the death of God's Son, Jesus Christ.

Reconciliation. In the social realm, reconciliation has occurred through the death of Jesus Christ. The

> God was willing to go to the point of death in order to bring humans into a reconciled relationship.

image here is of those who are estranged from each other coming together after a dispute. Hostilities are ended; friendship is established. This is what Jesus' death on the cross accomplished (Rom. 5:10; Col. 1:21–22). God has reconciled sinful humans both to God and to one another. Relationships are changed. Sinners have been reconciled with the One against whom they have sinned. Adversaries have been made friends, and peace is established where before enmity had existed. This change brings the most far-reaching effects. With social relationships changed, the world becomes "new"—like a "new creation" (2 Cor. 5:16–21). We are friends again with God and live in peace (Eph. 2:14–16).

Liberation. There is the image of liberation from the military realm. Humans are imprisoned by the powers of evil and sin; Jesus in his death has overcome evil powers and brought liberation—a great freedom. Jesus' resurrection after his death on the cross is God's divine victory over the powers of sin and evil that hold humans captive. Jesus is Lord means no human is lord over us—only Jesus is Lord. This is liberating to all who are oppressed and live—as African Americans did in the United States—under masters and lords who persecuted them. The death of Christ brings the triumph of love over hatred, of God's purposes for the world over the enslaving principalities and powers that would keep the world and all people within its grasp and turn every life away from God's purposes. Through Jesus' death liberation happens. The stranglehold of hatred is broken, the power of evil to kill and destroy has been overcome. This liberation can free us from the supremacy of sin in our lives and in the life of the world. Jesus is victor!

Expiation. There is the image of expiation from the religious realm. Humans are unclean, having become impure by their sins. We have not lived up to God's laws, and by our sinful actions we feel the stain of our impurity in the sight of God, who is holy and just and the standard by which our lives are judged. When we experience the guilt that our sin brings, that "aftertaste" that may leave us with a "guilty conscience," we know what it means to be in need of making amends or reparation or the forgiveness of mercy. We need someone who can purify us and make us clean in God's sight. In the cross of Jesus Christ we see God's Son, who died for us. God accepts Christ's holiness as the sacrifice for our sins. Jesus, who was holy and righteous, offers himself for our unholiness and unrighteousness. He cleanses us from sin and guilt. Jesus acts as our "high priest," to offer himself on our behalf and to offer his righteousness for our sinfulness. The purity of Jesus absorbs our impurity so that we, who are impure, can be forgiven and know peace with God. Jesus sacrifices himself for us.

Redemption. From the economic realm, there is the image of redemption. Here humans are portrayed as enslaved to the power of sin in their lives. They have no freedom of will and cannot but obey their impulses always to sin. Sin is an addiction, a power that we cannot shake or break in our lives. This sin affects everything we do, it enslaves us to its power. We break God's laws regularly by our own sinful choices. We accumulate sins because we act out of our nature as sinful human beings. We are powerless to help ourselves or to turn our lives in new directions. But God has acted through the death of Jesus Christ. Jesus' death is a "ransom" on our behalf. That is, Jesus offers his own obedience in the place of our disobedience. He breaks the addictive power of sin and death, to set us free from the power of sins in our lives. This is like what is sometimes called an "intervention" for those suffering from addictive behavior. But Jesus' death brings with it the power to make us new persons

> The "wonderful exchange" is that the righteous one, Jesus Christ, has taken on our unrighteousness, so that we—the unrighteous—may be redeemed and made righteous in God's sight. Jesus died to redeem us from sin.

and to give us a new power for living. We are redeemed. This is what is sometimes called the "wonderful exchange." Jesus' obedience to God's law and his faithfulness to God's will is the means God accepts to redeem us and to make us righteous in God's sight. The "wonderful exchange" is that the righteous one, Jesus Christ, has taken on our unrighteousness, so that we—the unrighteous—may be redeemed and made righteous in God's sight. Jesus died to redeem us from sin.

Justification. Then there is the image from the legal realm, justification. In the letters of the apostle Paul, particularly, humanity is portrayed as guilty before God. We are guilty as sinners because we have broken God's laws. We don't move very far down on the list of the Ten Commandments before we find that we are not perfect and have not kept the will of God the way God desires. We are sinners. Even worse, we deserve punishment for our sin. Our punishment, or judgment, is the result of our disobedience. God is our creator, and we are created for obedience. Since we disobey, we are guilty and deserve God's righteous judgments against our sin. God is holy and just. We are impure and sinful. But since we are guilty, we cannot rid ourselves of our own guilt. We cannot "pick ourselves up by our own bootstraps" and set ourselves in a right relation with God. How can we, since we are captive to the power of sin? So we need an outside helper. We need someone to take on our guilt, to act on our behalf and remove from us the curse of God's law—the law that shows us our guilt. This someone is Jesus Christ, who has died on the cross. God accepts his righteousness for our own unrighteousness, his innocence for our guilt, his obedience for our disobedience. By faith, we accept this work of Christ as being done for us, on our behalf. God forgives our sin. We are justified, we are saved by this work of Jesus Christ. The just Judge pronounces us innocent instead of guilty—because the righteousness of Jesus Christ is given to us. This is forgiveness; this is justification; this is salvation.

These are a number of the biblical images that relate to sin and salvation. Our sinful human condition is remedied by the work of Jesus Christ. Our old life is the life of sin; our new life is the life of salvation. Theologians have taken these biblical images of sin and salvation and have constructed theories of the atonement to explain more fully *how* the death of Christ brings forgiveness, liberation, expiation, redemption, and justification. There has been no one theory of the atonement that has ever been accepted by the whole Christian church as the only way to describe how salvation occurs by the death of Jesus Christ on the cross. The cross is so deep, so rich, that no one way of explaining it can exhaust its meaning. A theologian at the beginning of the last century said that the reason there was darkness over the earth from noon to three in the afternoon when Jesus hung on the cross (Matt. 27:45) was so that no persons could go home and say that they had "seen it all." No one can "see it all" or "say it all" when it comes to the atonement. Jesus Christ has died for our sins. This is the New Testament affirmation (Rom. 5:8). How God does this is a divine mystery. What is clear is the motivation. God accepts the death of Christ as the means for our salvation because of God's divine love for the world and for each of us. As the Bible's most famous verse puts it: "For God so loved the world that he gave his only Son, so that everyone who believes in him may not perish but may have eternal life" (John 3:16).

Resurrection of Jesus Christ

The central symbol of Christianity is the cross. The central fact of Christianity is the resurrection of Jesus Christ. In the Apostles' Creed, after we confess that Jesus was "crucified, dead, and buried" and "descended into hell," we also affirm that "on the third day he rose again from the dead." This unique affirmation sets Christianity apart from other religions and sets Jesus Christ apart from all others who ever lived. He died but was raised again from the dead—by the power of God.

There are always a number of questions that surround the resurrection of Jesus. Was the tomb really empty on that first Easter morning? Where did Jesus' body go? What was Jesus' resurrection body like? There are many answers we simply do not have. The Bible does not intend to give us the kind of historical and scientific information that will answer everything that "inquiring minds want to know"! Instead it presents us with narrative stories of Jesus' resurrection on the Sunday morning after his death on Friday (Matt. 28:1–15; Mark 16:1–8; Luke 24:1–12;

John 20:1–10), of his appearance to a group of women at the tomb where he had been laid, his later appearances at various points to his disciples, and then his ascension into heaven (Mark 16:19–20; Luke 24:50–53; Acts 1:6–11), after which time his resurrection appearances ceased.

The amazing story of the early Christian church is the story of those countless women and men who believed the truth of the resurrection accounts and experienced firsthand, for themselves, the presence of the risen Jesus Christ in their lives. They knew the reality of Christ's presence and power as their companions through the journey of life. They believed this and, even more, they were willing to give up their own lives as a witness to the truth that Jesus Christ is risen. This has been the key factor for Christianity in the two thousand years since: Christ is alive! He has been raised from the dead by the power of God.

Why does this matter and what does it mean? Presbyterians take to heart the answer of the Heidelberg Catechism:

Q. 45 How does Christ's resurrection benefit us?

A. First, by his resurrection he has overcome death, so that he might make us share in the righteousness he obtained for us by his death. Second, by his power we too are already raised to a new life. Third, Christ's resurrection is a sure pledge to us of our blessed resurrection. (*BC* 4.045)

The resurrection of Christ is not just a miracle that happened centuries ago, and that's that. It is a mighty work of God that continues to have ongoing, life-giving effects for us today. The resurrection marks Christ's power over death. The powers of sin and death and evil that led Christ to the cross are now defeated in his resurrection. God's triumphant power of love is stronger than the powers that seek to defeat it. Christ's resurrection enables us as believers in him to share the victory of salvation that he has accomplished—forgiveness, reconciliation, liberation, and all the other ways of expressing our new life: from sin to salvation.

Relatedly, says the Heidelberg Catechism, we also are raised by Christ's power to a new life. The same power of God that raised Jesus from the dead is able to raise us to new life—no matter how bad our circumstances, no matter how deep our sin, no matter what we have done in our lives that has been counter to God's will and purposes. New life in Christ means forgiveness and release from sin's power. It is the promise of God's presence with us now in Christ, so that sin can be resisted and so we can live the kind of loving, trusting, and obedient life that God intends us to experience.

Also, the resurrection of Christ benefits us by being the "sure pledge to us of our blessed resurrection." Christ's resurrection is the promise and guarantee that our physical death does not mark the end of our lives and our relationship with God. We have "eternal life"—a life lived forever in the presence of God in heaven—because Jesus Christ is raised from the dead. God's power in raising Christ from the dead is the same power that will raise us up to eternal life, a life of blessedness for eternity (1 Cor. 15:12–28). The resurrection of Christ shows God's power to overcome evil, suffering, sin, and death (Eph. 1:10; Phil. 3:10; 1 Pet. 1:3). This power is now ours in Jesus Christ. His resurrection is the assurance of our own. Our relationship with God is not ended with our physical death. Death is not a period at the end of life's sentence. It is just a comma, raising us to a new level of existence in the presence of the eternal God. As the hymn puts it: "Because he lives, we too, we too shall live"!

The Work of Christ

Why did God send Jesus Christ into the world? We wonder. Perhaps there are many reasons. But we recognize as we read the New Testament that the person and the work of Christ are inseparably connected. Who Jesus was expressed itself in what Jesus did. Jesus was able to do what he did because of who he was. Jesus did not just preach and teach. He also acted. We understand the actions of Jesus on the basis of what he said and who he was.

Presbyterians often look at the work of Christ in a threefold way: the three "offices" that Christ has carried out are the offices of prophet, priest, and king. They are three ways of understanding the big picture of who Jesus was and what he did.

Prophet. Jesus has been a prophet. Like the prophets in the Old Testament, Jesus announced the will and purposes of God. Jesus was a teacher. He taught us what God is like, what God wants of us as humans, and what God promises to do and be for us. Jesus announced that the reign, or kingdom, of God has now become a reality here on earth. He announces that, in his own self and in his ministries, the kingdom of God has dawned and come near. Jesus is our prophet.

Priest. Jesus has also been our priest. In his death on the cross, Jesus has died for us by offering himself as the sacrifice for our sins. Instead of our dying for our own sins—as punishment for what we have done or as the consequence of our own sinful actions—Jesus has suffered and died in our place. This is at the center of our faith: that Jesus has offered up his own self on our behalf. His death is sometimes called a "vicarious" death. The New Testament images of sin and salvation point us to this truth. Jesus died on our behalf. He died so that we can live. God accepts the sacrifice of Jesus as the offering for sin—just as in the Old Testament an animal was sacrificed on behalf of the sins of the people. So, now, we have a greater sacrifice—the sacrifice of God's own Son to be our sin offering to God. God accepts that death of Jesus as being offered for us, on our account. Through Jesus' death we have forgiveness. Through Jesus' death, we are reconciled with God. Our sin is forgiven and our lives are made new. Jesus is our priest.

King. Jesus is also our king. In biblical usage, "king" is the one who governs. The king has power and authority. The king is the one to whom allegiance and obedience are due. Jesus Christ is our king. After his death on the cross, Jesus was raised from the dead. In his resurrection, Jesus shows that God's power is the supreme power in the universe. In the resurrection, the power of sin and death are broken. Jesus suffered on the cross, was dead, and was buried. But on the third day God raised Jesus from the dead by God's own power. From that point on, it was clear that no power in the whole universe could ultimately defeat God's power in Jesus Christ. The strongest power in the universe to counter God's is the power of evil and sin and death. All of these had "done their worst," as the hymn puts it. They had put to death the innocent Son of God. But God's power had triumphed in the resurrection. Jesus Christ was raised from the dead by the power of God. Now Jesus Christ rules and reigns over the whole world. In his ascension, some forty days after his resurrection, Jesus is portrayed as being raised from the earth and as being raised to sit at the right hand of God (Acts 1). From that position—that position of authority and power—the risen, ascended Jesus Christ rules the world. The reign and kingdom about which Jesus

> The work of Jesus Christ is not a detached work. His life, death, and resurrection have the most personal of all effects.

spoke when he was on earth, that kingdom is now at work in this world, and will ultimately be established in all its fullness and power. Jesus Christ is our king.

Jesus is prophet, priest, and king. Those are three images that Reformed theology has emphasized as a way of encompassing the work of Jesus Christ as the incarnate Son of God, who died for our sins and was resurrected by the power of God, risen to rule the world through love. There is a certain flow in these three images. Jesus was a prophet throughout his life and ministry; he was a priest in his suffering (passion) and death; he is king through his resurrection and ascension. But in addition to the sequence, there is also a personal sense through these three images. Jesus is a prophet in speaking the divine Word of God's will *to* us. He is a priest in interceding *for* us. He is a king in ruling *over* us. What this means is that the work of Jesus Christ is not a detached work. His life, death, and resurrection have the most personal of all effects. They were all given *on our behalf.* For Jesus came to save "people like us." And all his actions and activities were carried out so that the good news of salvation can be proclaimed to the whole world.

Questions for Discussion

1. Why is it important for Christianity to believe in the doctrine of the incarnation?
2. Why is it important for Christianity to affirm that Jesus was "truly divine and truly human"?
3. Which images of sin and salvation are most meaningful to you?
4. What is the significance for Christian faith of the resurrection of Jesus Christ ?
5. In what ways can Presbyterians present Jesus Christ to our neighbors and society?

8

Holy Spirit

We have discussed the God who reveals, creates, and guides, as well as the Christ who saves people like us. But there is a third member of the Trinity, the Holy Spirit. The Holy Spirit shares fully the Godhead of the Father and the Son. The Spirit is active in all the works of the Godhead.

We have said that salvation comes to us in Jesus Christ, through the work of Christ. As we indicated, there are various biblical images used to describe the sinful human condition. There are also various biblical images used to describe the salvation that comes to us in and through Jesus Christ. In the Presbyterian tradition, Christ's work is seen as prophet, priest, and king—as a way of describing the fullness of what Jesus Christ has done.

But behind all the ways of describing salvation there is the Holy Spirit. Presbyterian theology has seen the crucial role the Holy Spirit plays in salvation to be an especially important conviction. It is the Spirit who grants the gift of faith. The Spirit is the one who initiates faith, nurtures faith, and brings faith to fruition. This is crucial, because faith is the means by which we as human beings come to an awareness of our sinfulness and of God's gracious provision of salvation in Jesus Christ. The Holy Spirit is the one who makes faith possible. The Spirit is God at work within us. Sometimes a distinction is made between the "objective" work of Christ and the "subjective" work. The "objective work" is Christ's life, death, resurrection, and ascension—that which Jesus Christ has done, or what God has done in and through Jesus Christ. The "subjective work" is our own personal, human appropriation of this objective work. It is the work of Jesus Christ becoming "real" to us. It is our recognition of our need for salvation and our accepting the work of Jesus Christ by faith as having been done *for us*. It is the subjective work—making salvation real—that is the work of the Holy Spirit.

The Holy Spirit in Scripture is portrayed as doing many things. The Spirit is at work in God's creation of the world and in God's preserving the world and all of human life (Gen. 1:2; 2:7; Ps. 104:30). The word "spirit," in both the Hebrew language in which the Old Testament was written and the Greek language in which the New Testament was written, literally means "breath." God's breath is God's Spirit. God's Spirit, or breath, gives life to all things. When we see life—wherever we find it—we know God's Spirit is operative.

The Holy Spirit is active in the world. God's Spirit brings forth human wisdom, culture, creativity, and wisdom (Exod. 31:1–5; 35:31; Job 32:8; Dan. 1:17). God's Spirit is operative both in human communities and among individual people. God's Spirit inspired the Scriptures; the Spirit helps interpret the Scriptures; and God's Spirit brings forth faith in Jesus Christ. God's Spirit is also God's ongoing presence in the lives of the Christian community (the church) and in the lives of individual Christian believers. So the Spirit is tremendously active in all times and places.

The Spirit and Scripture

It is especially important to recognize the work of the Spirit in relation to Holy Scripture. We spoke above about the Scriptures as the Word of God, the place in which God's revelation or self-communication is given. This is what makes the Bible unique and authoritative for Christians. But how do we come to this conviction? What leads us to confess that the Scriptures are not just one

> Presbyterian theology has always understood that we can confess our recognition of Scripture as the Word of God only when the Holy Spirit illumines us, or enlightens us.

book among many but are the Word of God? Presbyterian theology has always understood that we can confess our recognition of Scripture as the Word of God only when the Holy Spirit illumines us, or enlightens us. Theologians refer to this as the "internal witness," or the "internal testimony of the Holy Spirit." What this means is simply that as we read the Bible, it is by the work of the Spirit of God that we are led to encounter God in Jesus Christ in the Scriptures. The Holy Spirit "testifies" or "witnesses" to Jesus Christ as our Lord and Savior and also to the conviction that the Scriptures are God's revelation. Through the witness of the Spirit we come to believe that God is the ultimate author of Scripture. We hear God's divine Word through the human words of the biblical writers of Scripture by the work of the Holy Spirit.

The Spirit and Salvation

The Spirit "illumines" or "enlightens" us to confess Jesus Christ as our Lord and Savior. The picture here is one of helping us to see, or making this conviction clear to us. The image is apt. One of the effects of sin on human beings is to blind us to the reality of God. Sin corrupts our hearts and turns our vision away from God and inwardly toward ourselves, with our own wants and desires.

The Holy Spirit "opens our eyes." Through the witness of the Spirit within us, we are given the gift of faith so that we now see Jesus Christ for who he really is: our Lord and Savior. This "enlightenment"

> The Holy Spirit "opens our eyes." Through the witness of the Spirit within us, we are given the gift of faith so that we now see Jesus Christ for who he really is: our Lord and Savior.

is God's work within us, by the Spirit. By our own power, we are not capable of coming to faith on our own, or removing the blinders from our eyes. The power of sin is too great and pervasive. It is only God through the Holy Spirit who is able to work within us and give us this new sight. By the Spirit we see Jesus for who he is and we see the Scriptures for what they are—God's divine revelation to us. Without the Holy Spirit at work within us, we would be unable to believe the Christian gospel. The work of the Spirit "turns the lights on" for us, enabling us to see Jesus Christ, and indeed God's whole creation, with new eyes—the eyes of faith.

The Spirit "opens" our eyes and our hearts. The Holy Spirit gives us the gift of faith, which is the means by which our salvation is made real to us. By faith we appropriate, or make personal, the work of Jesus Christ—his death and his resurrection. The Spirit gives faith and thus makes us a "new creation" (2 Cor. 5:17). We move from sin to salvation, from "death" to "life" (1 John 3:14). We are drawn to Christ by the work of God through the Holy Spirit (John 6:44). Theologically, this is called "regeneration." This is God's work of transformation within us. In regeneration, the Holy Spirit gives us a "new birth," or "birth from above" (John 3:3) and salvation through Jesus Christ (Titus 3:5). The Spirit makes the work of Christ real to us by giving us new hearts and minds. The Spirit overcomes the power of sin that enslaves us and affects the totality of our lives by making us into new people. The power of sin is broken in our lives through the work of Christ, which we understand and embrace and love by the work of the Holy Spirit within us. Our hearts, minds, and whole existence are transformed so totally that the images of "new birth" and "new creation" are most appropriate. Now we love God, love Jesus Christ, trust in him, and seek to do his will instead of living life "turned in upon ourselves" and seeking only our own good. The Holy Spirit is the agent of salvation.

Presbyterian theology stresses the role of the Holy Spirit in salvation. It is only by the work of the Spirit that salvation can become real to us. The Spirit "testifies" or "witnesses" to the work of Jesus Christ, whom God sent to live, die, and be raised again for our salvation (1 Cor. 12:3).

Questions for Discussion

1. Do you often think of the Holy Spirit as present in your life? Why, or why not?

2. What examples do you see in the world around us of the Holy Spirit's work?
3. Why is it important to recognize the role of the Holy Spirit in leading us to believe the Scriptures are God's Word?
4. In what ways may the Holy Spirit lead us to have faith in Jesus Christ?
5. Do you think Presbyterians give enough emphasis to the Holy Spirit today? Why, or why not?

9

Election and Predestination

*P*resbyterian theology specially stresses that it is through the work of the Holy Spirit that we come to have faith in Jesus Christ. The Spirit calls together God's people in the community of faith we call the church. To see these important points helps us deal best with a doctrine for which the Reformed tradition—and especially Presbyterians—is well known. This is the doctrine of predestination, or election.

There are many common caricatures of the doctrine of predestination. Sometimes it is said that the doctrine turns people into puppets, because they have no freedom of choice and are just playing out a divinely ordained "script" in life—freedom to choose is an illusion. Sometimes predestination is said to make God into a tyrant, reserving salvation for only a select few people. At other points, the doctrine of election has been criticized as cutting the nerve of evangelism or making it so that Christians think that because they are of the "elect" they can simply coast along in the Christian life and do not have to conform. Sometimes "election" has been translated as "elitism," making some people think they are "better" than others.

Theologically, Presbyterians believe that these critiques are not accurate, though not all Presbyterians hold to exactly the same views on election and predestination. The views of John Calvin, the views of Calvin's followers in the seventeenth century (called Reformed orthodoxy), and in the twentieth century the views of the Swiss Reformed theologian Karl Barth (1886–1968) have all presented these doctrines in ways that display some differences.

What follows here leans most heavily on Calvin and the Reformed confessions, the views that have been most influential historically among Presbyterians.

The terms "election" and "predestination" are often used synonymously. They refer to God's work in salvation.

This is a doctrine that is much maligned and caricatured. In the Presbyterian tradition, the doctrine of predestination has been developed in several ways. At its base, it goes back to the views of John Calvin in the sixteenth century (and beyond him to the theologian Augustine in the fourth century). But the doctrine was also developed after the time of Calvin, in the seventeenth century in a form that to some sounds very harsh. This formulation is found in the Westminster Confession of Faith. It speaks of God's eternal decrees, by which God "for the manifestation of his glory" has predestinated some persons and angels to "everlasting life" while others are "fore-ordained to everlasting death" (*BC* 6.016). God has chosen in Christ those who, out of God's "free grace and love alone," are "elected" to salvation while from others God has withheld mercy, choosing to pass them by and "to ordain them to dishonour and wrath for their sin" (*BC* 6.020). Thus there are the elect and the nonelect. The elect are chosen by God's grace for salvation; others are passed over and receive the results of their own sinful actions, which are judgment and God's wrath.

> The terms "election" and "predestination" are often used synonymously. They refer to God's work in salvation.

This is a view of predestination that has been very influential in Presbyterian history. Other confessions in our tradition do not go into as much detail on the doctrine. Other confessions do not deal with this doctrine in the sections that consider God's actions in eternity, as does the Westminster Confession. Instead, these confessions (and Calvin himself in his *Institutes of the Christian Religion*) deal with the doctrine of election or predestination in the context of salvation (soteriology), that is, how we are saved. The purpose of the doctrine of predestination is not to lead people to speculate on whether or not they are saved by God. If you think of God and God's actions, or what God may do (called theologically "God's decrees"), it is possible to think of God's making an absolute decree about who will be saved and who won't (as in the Westminster Confession, cited above). This action of God would be unknown to us as humans.

But consider the difference when you think of election in the context of the experience of salvation, of what God has done for us in Jesus Christ. Then the question is not what God has eternally decreed in the mysterious past, which is unknown to us. Now the question is: Will I accept the salvation in Jesus Christ with which I am confronted? Will I respond to God's gift of salvation in and through Jesus Christ? If I will, I realize that God has chosen me or "elected" me to come to faith by the power of the Holy Spirit.

For Calvin, the doctrine of predestination emerged out of a very practical situation. Why is it, he wondered, that some people believe in the Christian gospel and have faith, and others don't? This was a pastoral problem. Calvin's answer was that some people believed because God through the Holy Spirit granted them the gift of faith. This was God's election of these people to have faith and thus to be Christians. This is the work of God's election that the Scriptures speak about when, for example, the apostle Paul says in the book of Romans that "those whom [God] foreknew he also predestined to be conformed to the image of his Son" (Rom. 8:29), or in Eph. 1:11 that "in Christ we have also obtained an inheritance, having been destined according to the purpose of him who accomplishes all things according to his counsel and will." The emphasis is that it is God who elects and chooses persons in Jesus Christ. These are persons who exhibit the faith that comes as the gift of the Holy Spirit. When we see persons who have faith, we can be sure that it is the Holy Spirit who is operative and at work in their lives. We do not come to faith in Jesus Christ by ourselves. We come as a result of the Holy Spirit's work within us. If we believe, it is because God has graciously worked within us by the Spirit to enlighten us to believe in Jesus Christ and to "regenerate" our lives in Christ, so that we are a "new creation." Election, or predestination, is another way of saying that we are saved by God's grace.

This way of understanding election and predestination places the emphasis on the present and the future. We do not sit around speculating about whether or not God has elected us before all eternity to be saved—are we part of God's eternal decree of election? Instead, we focus on a very practical question. Quite simply, we ask ourselves: Do I believe in Jesus Christ? If we can answer in all sincerity: Yes, I believe; Jesus Christ is my Lord and Savior—then we can be assured of our election. Our response to Christ is the crucial question. Calvin called Christ the "mirror of election" (*Institutes* 3.24.5). As we look to him, we see God's loving purposes of salvation, and that through his death and resurrection we can share in the salvation God graciously gives. So our question about our election to salvation should be "christologically focused," or focused on Jesus Christ. The Second Helvetic Confession declares that "we are elected or predestinated in Christ" (*BC* 5.053). Do we believe in him as God's Son and our Lord and Savior? If so, we know that the Holy Spirit has been at work in our lives and has given us the gift of faith. Remember,

> We do not sit around speculating about whether or not God has elected us before all eternity to be saved. . . . We ask ourselves: Do I believe in Jesus Christ?

in Presbyterian theology humans are enslaved to the power of sin. We can do nothing *on our own* to create faith or to get rid of our sinful condition. If we are to be saved, it must be by the work of God, through the Holy Spirit, bringing us to faith in our savior Jesus Christ. So if we *do* have faith in Jesus Christ, we know that the Spirit is at work—and that we are elected by God. The Second Helvetic Confession puts it this way: "Let Christ, therefore be the looking glass, in whom we may contemplate our predestination. We shall have a sufficiently clear and sure testimony that we are inscribed in the Book of Life if we have fellowship with Christ, and he is ours and we are his in true faith" (*BC* 5.060).

The flip side of this is that just as we do not sit around speculating our own election, we do not conjecture about other people and whether they are "elect" or saved. Whether or not they are saved—this is God's decision. This is God's prerogative, to work within persons in whatever ways that God pleases. It is not our place to judge. It is not our place to speculate about their eternal destiny. Today a person may show no signs of Christian faith—tomorrow, God's Spirit may work in an unexpectedly powerful way to create faith and turn that person into a Christian! We simply do not know what God's Spirit is doing in people's lives. God's work among us is a mystery. We should be driven to praise and thanksgiving when faith is real and when God's Spirit is at work.

Election or predestination ought to be a supremely comforting doctrine. It points us to the fact that God is the one who saves us—not we ourselves. Our salvation comes from the work of God in our lives, by the Spirit who gives us faith in Jesus Christ. We do not and cannot save ourselves. This is really "good news"! The good news is that God can and does do for us that which we cannot do for ourselves—saves us. Our salvation does not depend on our own faith—how strong or much or deep our faith is. Our salvation depends on God's gift of faith to us, God's perfect gift, which is able to bring us new lives in Jesus Christ and a new relationship with God and with other people. Our comfort and assurance is that salvation depends on God, not on us. Our only question is: Do I believe in Jesus Christ? If we can answer that we do, we *know* that God's Spirit has created faith within us and that we abide in Christ (1 John 3:24; John 15:4–5). Our salvation is assured by this work of God—not our own.

> Election or predestination ought to be a supremely comforting doctrine. It points us to the fact that God is the one who saves us—not we ourselves.

Questions for Discussion

1. Why is it important for Presbyterians to affirm that our salvation is due solely to God's electing grace?
2. In what ways is it helpful to think of election as focused on the question: "Do I believe in Jesus Christ?"

3. In what ways can election and predestination lead to vigorous evangelism? In what ways can election and predestination keep us from judging others?
4. Do you think God is obliged either to "save" or to "condemn" all people?
5. What comforts and challenges do you find in the doctrine of election?

10

Salvation by Grace

God's gracious election means that we are saved by God's grace. God's grace is the pure, unmerited favor of God, given to us without any preconditions or human achievements. Grace is God's gift. That we are saved by God's grace means that we are saved solely by God's good favor toward us—not by any works we do or by anything we have achieved or by how pure we try to make ourselves be. We are saved by God's grace given to us in Jesus Christ. Our faith and belief in him is the means by which salvation by grace becomes a reality for us. As Paul put it: "For by grace you have been saved through faith, and this is not your own doing; it is the gift of God—not the result of works, so that no one may boast" (Eph. 2:8–9). Presbyterians see salvation by grace as a way of affirming God's election and predestination. We are adopted into the covenant family of God by the work of God in Jesus Christ, which comes to us as God's unmerited favor (grace) and not as the result of any efforts of our own (Gal. 4:4–5; Eph. 1:5).

> Presbyterians see salvation by grace as a way of affirming God's election and predestination.

The doctrine of "adoption" is an expression of this entry into God's covenant family (Rom. 8:15). Presbyterians stress that we receive the "grace of adoption" and "enjoy the liberties and privileges of the children of God" (*BC* 6.074). This act of God's grace means we belong to God, receive God's spirit, and can approach God as children approach their parents with "boldness and confidence" (Eph. 3:12; Rom. 5:2; Heb. 4:16). God has compassion for us (Ps. 103:13), protects us (Ps. 27:1–3), provides for us (Matt. 6:30), cares for us (1 Pet. 5:7), and at times disciplines us (Heb. 12:6). Yet we are never forsaken by God (Ps. 94:14; Heb. 13:5). Instead, we are "marked with a seal for the day of redemption" (Eph. 4:30) and inherit the wonderful promises of God (Heb. 6:12) as those who receive eternal salvation (2 Tim. 2:10; 1 Pet. 1:4; Heb. 1:14).

Salvation by God's grace works itself out in a number of ways. Our lives as Christian people are the constant exploration and wonder at what God has done, is doing, and will do in our lives by the power of the Holy Spirit. We are constantly aware that all we are and all we have come from God. We experience God's gracious blessings in our lives and see God's providential leading, guiding us through all our experiences. For this, our attitudes are gratitude and praise to God.

A distinctive dimension of being a Presbyterian Christian is our understanding and recognition of God's work in our lives, in salvation, and in our whole Christian existence. To see this, we can examine some steps in salvation. These are expressed by words that belong in the vocabulary of Christian theology and of Christian experience. These are theological terms that Presbyterians share in common with other Christians and other traditions. But our Presbyterian beliefs see these terms in relation to each other in some ways that are distinctive from other traditions. This does not drive us away from Christian fellowship or mutual love with other Christians. Instead it points us toward the ways in which our Presbyterian beliefs are a particular expression of the Christian gospel and the emphases that help make Presbyterian beliefs distinctive. Here are some of these "steps in salvation."

God's Initiative

A basic instinct of Presbyterian belief is that God is the one who takes the initiative. We saw this from the very beginning—in revelation, God chooses to be revealed. In creation, God chooses to establish a universe, a world, and to create people. So also in salvation, in election and predestination, it is God who chooses to save persons, out of divine love and mercy.

As we experience salvation, we are aware that God is at work and that God has been at work within us. Long before we are conscious of believing in Jesus Christ, we recognize that God has been preparing our lives to come to faith in Jesus Christ. If we have been baptized as infants, we realize that in baptism God has been reaching out to draw us into the covenant community through the church and our parents. Theologians sometimes call this "prevenient grace," or the "grace that goes before" our believing. This "preparatory grace" is the work of God long before we believe. It is an expression of God's electing love.

Our salvation by God's grace as an expression of God's election, while rooted in God's eternal love and mercy, takes shape for us in the lives we live. Some people are very clear on the exact instant or time at which they came to have faith in Jesus Christ. They have an experience that is very real and vivid. For others, coming to faith in Jesus Christ as Lord and Savior is a gradual or ongoing direction in life that takes shape over many years. At some point, one looks back and may say, "I don't remember a time when I wasn't a Christian." In either case, we are aware that we have come to faith in Jesus Christ and that we have done so by God's love and power in us.

Regeneration

Presbyterians have recognized that, for salvation to take root within us, "regeneration" is a starting point. What does this mean? "Regeneration" is a theological term that comes from the Latin term *regeneratio,* meaning "new birth" or "new life." Regeneration is the action of the Holy Spirit,

> Regeneration is the action of the Holy Spirit, who transforms our lives by giving us the gift of faith so that we experience a "new birth" or "new life" in Jesus Christ.

who transforms our lives by giving us the gift of faith so that we experience a "new birth" or "new life" in Jesus Christ— or so that we experience "salvation" (Titus 3:5). In a broad sense, our whole Christian experience, as we reflect upon it, is "regeneration." We have passed from "death" into "life" (John 5:24; Rom. 6:13; 1 John 3:14). We experience our "death" to sin and become "alive" to a new existence in Jesus Christ. We become aware of our sin, recognize Jesus Christ as the one who has died for our sins, accept his love and forgiveness, and experience the "new creation" as "everything old has passed away" and "everything has become new!" (2 Cor. 5:17). God's grace has not "fixed up" our old self; God has made us new beings.

"Regeneration" is our way of referring to what God has done within us by the power of the Holy Spirit. God opens our eyes, opens our ears, and implants the gift of faith within us so that we can receive the benefits of salvation given through the cross and resurrection of Jesus Christ. This is something we cannot do for ourselves because of our sin. So God has taken the initiative and in gracious election "regenerates" us by giving the sheer gift of new life within us.

Conversion

A second step in our salvation is conversion. Conversion means "turning around." It is our conscious response to God's regenerating work within us. It is our facing a new direction, our act of consciously willing to try to live as a disciple and servant of Jesus Christ.

Our "conversion" is our change of consciousness. It is our conscious orienting of our lives into the new direction of love and service to Jesus Christ.

There are many ways in which people become "converted." God can use many means to give us the gift of faith in Christ and to bring us to the point where we turn around and face a new direction in life. Most often this occurs through the preaching of the Word of God. As Jesus Christ is proclaimed as God's Son, our Lord and Savior, the Holy Spirit gives the gift of faith in regeneration and persons believe and are converted. This is what the New Testament portrays as happening in many instances when preachers preach: crowds of people as well as individuals believe the gospel, or "good news," that God has come into the world to save the world in Jesus Christ (John 3:16; Acts 2:38). At other times, people may be "converted" as they read the Scriptures or discuss Jesus Christ with their neighbors (Acts 8:26–40). Our "conversion" is our change of consciousness. It is our conscious orienting of our lives into the new direction of love and service to Jesus Christ.

Repentance

Our conversion, or turning, has two parts. The first is repentance. We've all heard the cry: "Repent!" Repentance is a biblical term that means a change in our minds and life direction. It means sorrow for our sin, contrition for what we have done wrong in God's sight. It means that "the wicked forsake their way, and the unrighteous their thoughts" (Isa. 55:7). When John the Baptist proclaimed a "baptism of repentance," he said people should "bear fruits worthy of repentance." In response to the question of what people should do, John said, "Whoever has two coats must share with anyone who has none; and whoever has food must do likewise" (Luke 3:1–14; cf. Acts 26:20). A new way of living—of sharing instead of hoarding, for example—is an initial step of repentance. Repentance is the first part of conversion. It marks our desire to live out the new direction toward which our conversion has oriented us. We renounce the ways of sin in which we have lived and look forward to the ways of living that God now calls us toward as followers of Jesus Christ. Our grief over our sin "produces a repentance that leads to salvation" (2 Cor. 7:10). In repentance we receive God's forgiveness for our sins, the inward cleansing by the Holy Spirit, so that our sorrow for sin resolves to express itself in living with a new agenda: being a disciple of Jesus Christ, loving and serving him.

Faith

The second part of conversion is faith. In addition to our sorrow for sin and our resolve to have our lives "turned around" to walk in a new direction, we look forward by faith. In salvation, everything depends on faith, just as everything also depends on God's grace. Our salvation comes by grace *through* faith. Faith is the means by which our regeneration is realized, by which our conversion takes shape. Faith is trust, our appropriation of the death of Jesus Christ on the cross as being the means by which God forgives our sin and establishes us in salvation with a new relationship to God and to others. Faith is the way by which our conversion is expressed. Faith is the gift of the Holy Spirit that enables us to receive the benefits of salvation as being for us. Faith is the attitude the Spirit implants within us to be able to trust Jesus Christ for salvation and to live our lives in obedience to his will and guidance.

Faith is the attitude the Spirit implants within us to be able to trust Jesus Christ for salvation and to live our lives in obedience to his will and guidance.

Faith is a revolutionary quality because it marks our way of living life. It affects all aspects of our life. Our faith in Jesus Christ reorients our minds, our emotions, and our actions (our heads, hearts, and hands).

By faith we apprehend what God has done for us in Christ. John Calvin defined faith as "a firm and certain knowledge of God's benevolence toward us" (*Institutes* 3.1.4). Through faith we gain a certain knowledge of God's being "for us" in Jesus Christ, of the forgiveness of sins in Jesus Christ. We can know and believe that "while we still were sinners Christ died for us" and that this is the proof of God's love (Rom. 5:8). So our minds are radically realigned! We are no longer God's enemies—we are reconciled by the cross of Christ (Eph. 2:1–10; Col. 1:20; 2:14). We believe our lives are meaningful and have a purpose. We believe that God has come to live among us and show us how to live. God's truth has become a person in Jesus Christ, who is "the way, and the truth, and the life" (John 14:6).

Our emotions and our desires are also revolutionized by faith in Jesus Christ. When we realize the immensity of God's grace, the depth of God's love in the cross of Christ, and the power of Christ's resurrection to conquer sin and death and to make real the promise of eternal life—we are staggered! Our hearts are transformed by the overwhelming sense of God's grace to claim us and renew us and bring us love, joy, and peace. As Paul put it, "Since we are justified by faith, we have peace with God through our Lord Jesus Christ" (Rom. 5:1). Our faith gives us the assurance that our lives are "hidden with Christ in God" (Col. 3:3) and that nothing in all creation—no powers, events, or evil—"will be able to separate us from the love of God in Christ Jesus our Lord" (Rom. 8:39).

The gift of faith also opens new meaning and purpose for our lives. We now live with an attitude of trust in God, instead of alienation. We now find the meaning and significance of our existence in being children of God, adopted into God's family, and living according to God's will in Christ, rather than seeking meaning in ourselves and our own achievements. Through faith we can live in freedom from sin and guilt, serving Christ and others completely in this world through all our efforts, rather than trying only to amass more and more to promote ourselves.

Union with Christ

Salvation has come to us by God's grace. Through faith we are united with Jesus Christ by the power of the Holy Spirit. This union with Christ is the fundamental relationship that Christian people have in salvation. Jesus spoke of his being the vine and his disciples being the branches and said, "Abide in me as I abide in you" (John 15:4–5). Those who have a relationship with Jesus Christ by faith are members of a body, with Christ as their head (Eph. 4:15–16). Calvin put it simply when he wrote: "Christ, when he illumines us into faith by the power of his Spirit, at the same time so engrafts us into his body that we become partakers of every good" (*Institutes* 3.2.35). Our union with Christ by faith is the way we participate in the benefits that Christ has won for us in salvation. This is a personal union, through which we experience Christ's presence as the "indwelling of Christ in our heart" (*Institutes* 3.11.10). This is sometimes called a "mystical union." We experience Christ's presence and his benefits so that "Christ, having been made ours, makes us sharers with him in the gifts with which he has been endowed. . . . We put on Christ and are engrafted into his body. . . . He deigns to make us one with him" (*Institutes* 3.11.10). This language speaks as strongly as possible of the believer's union with Christ being so deep and intimate that his righteousness overcomes our sin and he lives in us as we live in him. This is the sentiment expressed by Paul, who wrote: "I have been crucified with Christ; and it is no longer I who live, but it is Christ who lives in me. And the life I now live in the flesh I live by faith in the Son of God, who loved me and gave himself for me" (Gal. 2:19–20). Our union with Christ by faith is the deepest reality we can know and the most important relationship that we can ever have.

> "We put on Christ and are engrafted into his body. . . . He deigns to make us one with him." —John Calvin

Salvation by Faith

Our union with Christ through faith is our salvation. Faith is the means by which salvation is made real to us. During the Protestant Reformation in the sixteenth century, one of the key insights of Martin Luther (1483–1546) and of Reformed theologians after him was that we are saved by "faith alone." This means that it is solely on the basis of faith in Jesus Christ that salvation is received. We as humans cannot do anything at all to merit it, or earn it, or achieve it. We are "justified by faith" (Rom. 5:1) on the basis of God's grace alone.

The Protestant Reformers believed the Roman Catholic Church

of the day was teaching that salvation is achieved by faith—defined as believing what the church taught—plus "good works." The good works were ways of gaining merit in the sight of God. Believers cooperated in their salvation by contributing their "part" as they did works to accumulate merit before God. This gave rise to the perennially popular notion that if you "live a good life" and do "good works," you will go to heaven when you die.

Presbyterians, along with other Protestants, reject the formula Faith + Works → Salvation. On the basis of the New Testament and the way God has worked all through the Bible, we believe that we are set right, or "justified," in God's sight not by any works we do but solely on the basis of the righteousness of Jesus Christ. Christ's death on the cross is the way in which God has reached out to save those who believe. We receive salvation as the free gift of God's grace through faith in Jesus Christ, given by the Holy Spirit. It is Christ alone who saves us, by God's grace alone, and through faith alone.

But salvation does not stop there. Presbyterians believe, again with other Protestants, that once we confess Jesus Christ as our Lord and Savior and are united with Christ by faith, our relationship with Christ will lead us into doing "good works" that serve Christ and give glory to God. We do these works of love, justice, and mercy out of gratitude for the salvation that is ours in Christ. We serve Christ and our neighbors in this world not *in order to* gain salvation but rather *as a result of* our salvation. Our good works in Christ's service show our loving response to the electing love that has granted us salvation through God's son. So, in our Protestant and Presbyterian tradition, the formula is: Salvation → Faith + Works. Our "works"

> To believe our salvation rests totally on God's electing grace and is freely given to us by the Holy Spirit who grants us faith in Jesus Christ frees us to live lives of joyful obedience in the world.

follow as our way of showing our thanksgiving to God. The Second Helvetic Confession notes that "works necessarily proceed from faith" (*BC* 5.119).We will obey God's law in order to show our commitment to following God's will, not as a means of trying to attain salvation by our own efforts.

Realizing the differences in these two approaches to salvation can make all the difference in the world to us. To believe our salvation rests totally on God's electing grace and is freely given to us by the Holy Spirit who grants us faith in Jesus Christ frees us to live lives of joyful obedience in the world. We still sin. Our "works" are never done "purely," from totally unselfish motives. But we confess our sins. We are forgiven by God. We repent. We live out the direction we turned to in conversion, resolving to turn away from sin and follow the way of Christ. We live, day by day, by the same faith that saves us through God's power at work within us (Eph. 3:20).

Perseverance

One of the distinctive views of Presbyterians is that those who believe in Jesus Christ for salvation will never lose their salvation. This is sometimes called "the perseverance of the saints" ("saints" is the New Testament designation for Christian believers, see, e.g., 1 Cor. 1:2; Eph. 1:1). Jesus said, "I give them eternal life, and they will never perish. No one will snatch them out of my hand" (see John 10:28–29). The continuous power of the Holy Spirit in believers is operative throughout our lives. The Spirit gave the gift of faith; the Spirit continues to be present in believers' lives; and the Spirit will bring to completion God's work of salvation in those who believe. This was the assurance of the apostle Paul who wrote, "I am confident of this, that the one who began a good work among you will bring it to completion by the day of Jesus Christ" (Phil. 1:6).

Other traditions, such as the Methodist and some Baptist traditions, teach that those who believe can lose their salvation through "backsliding" or apostasy, slipping into unbelief. Presbyterians believe that those who live in this manner, who may once have professed Christian faith and then later have rejected it, did not have genuine faith in Christ in the first place. Their "faith" was only "temporary." It was not the true faith that saves. We should never think we can sin indiscriminately because "once saved, always saved." We can't believe that we can "continue in sin in order that grace may abound" (Rom. 6:1). Of course not! That would only show the non-genuineness of our faith. But we can be sure that the God who has elected us and saved us will also hold us forever in the salvation given freely to us (Heb. 10:23).

The Work of God

While Presbyterians hold many agreements with other Christian traditions about the nature of salvation, there are also emphases that are distinctive in Reformed or Presbyterian beliefs.

One way to capsulize these is to recognize that Presbyterians also stress the initiating work of God. It is God who makes the "first move," and especially so in salvation. We have seen this in doctrines of revelation, incarnation, and election. So also in salvation as it is realized by the believer—it is God who acts prior to any action or activity on our parts. Presbyterians emphasize that regeneration precedes conversion and faith. We do not bring our "faith" *to* God, we receive faith *from* God through the Holy Spirit. It is God's work that regenerates us, converts us, leads us to repentance, and initiates faith within us. God's Spirit unites us with Jesus Christ to live lives of faith. God's own power sustains us so that God holds us in perseverance in faith unto eternal life. In salvation, all glory belongs to God. For "we are saved by grace and the favor of Christ alone" (*BC* 5.119).

Questions for Discussion

1. What is the importance of "salvation by grace" for Presbyterians?
2. Why do Presbyterians stress that salvation occurs from God's initiative?
3. Was there a definite point in your life when you consciously experienced "regeneration" or "conversion"?
4. What does "faith" mean to you?
5. What are the comforts and challenges in believing in God's work of "perseverance" in our salvation?

PART III

The Church, Where Faith Begins, Is Nourished, and Grows

11

Church

*T*he Holy Spirit of God creates faith in us and in others. The work of creating faith in many people is the Spirit's work of calling and gathering together the church of Jesus Christ. The church is a community of faith, the people of God who are drawn together across all lines of nationality, gender, or economic location by the common work of God's Spirit in creating faith. Faith is trust. Faith is receiving the free gift of salvation by God's grace. Faith is believing that Jesus Christ has died for my sins. Faith is our personal appropriation of the gospel message.

A Presbyterian view of the church stresses God's initiatives in establishing salvation and in calling those who have faith into one body—the church. This is how the gospel message of salvation is spread throughout the world.

We hear the gospel message in the context of the community of God, other people of faith—the Christian church. The church is the corporate body of believers, who are called by God and drawn together by the Holy Spirit to live as God's people and disciples of Jesus Christ in the world. A Presbyterian view of the church stresses God's initiatives in establishing salvation and in calling those who have faith into one body—the church. This is how the gospel message of salvation is spread throughout the world.

At our best, Presbyterians should be vigorous for evangelism. We are strong on evangelism, the proclamation of the gospel of Jesus Christ, because we recognize that it is by our witness in proclamation that the Holy Spirit can work to bring others to faith in Jesus Christ as Lord and Savior. We preach and teach the gospel vigorously, not because it is *by* our efforts that anyone will be saved, but it may well be *through* our efforts that salvation can come to be realized in someone's life. It is God, through the Holy Spirit in the church, that brings forth faith and brings others into the fellowship of the church with the body of Christian believers. So evangelism should be strong in our churches in the Reformed and Presbyterian tradition.

People of the Covenant

We hear the gospel message in the context of the church. We see ourselves in the church as the ongoing people of God, who continue to live out the covenant relationship that God has entered into with us, in Jesus Christ. Presbyterians emphasize that God has worked with people. In the Bible we see that God has sought community. God has established relationships with people. God has entered into those relationships by establishing covenants. Think of all the biblical covenants. There was the covenant with Noah, in which God promised never again to destroy the earth by floods (Gen. 6). There was the covenant with Abraham and Sarah, in which God promised them blessings and descendants (Gen. 12). There was the covenant God made with the people of Israel when the Law, the Ten Commandments, was given on Mount Sinai; God promised to be Israel's God and Israel promised to be God's people. There was the covenant with David, in which God promised a coming Messiah, through David's progeny (2 Sam. 7:1–17; 1 Kings 9:5; 1 Chr. 17:1–15; 2 Chr. 7:18). Supremely, there is the fulfillment of that covenant in the Messiah—who we Christians believe is Jesus Christ—who did emerge. Jesus referred to himself as the "new covenant"—the new way that God has related to human beings once and for all (Luke 22:20; 1 Cor. 11:25; cf. Jer. 31:31).

In the Christian church, we see ourselves as continuing to be the people of God, the new Israel, the covenant community of those joined together with each other and joined together with God through Jesus Christ. The church is God's covenant people, who by faith are united in Jesus Christ. Because of our faith, we seek to serve God as followers of our Lord and Savior Jesus Christ. We do not live the life of faith alone. True faith in Christ propels us into the fellowship of others who have also confessed Christ as their Lord. We find ourselves together as people of the covenant in the church—where faith begins and then is nourished and grows. There can be no "Lone Ranger" Christianity. No one can "go it alone" in the Christian life. Authentic Christian existence is to be drawn into the fellowship of others who also share the faith and are also committed to carrying out the mission and ministry of Jesus Christ in this world.

> The church is God's covenant people who by faith are united in Jesus Christ. Because of our faith, we seek to serve God as followers of our Lord and Savior Jesus Christ.

The Visible Church

The church as the body of believers we can see around us we call the "visible church." This is the church that opens its doors to all comers. Whoever confesses Jesus Christ as Lord and Savior is welcomed in the church. This is the only requirement for membership in Presbyterian churches: faith in Jesus Christ. When persons make a public profession of their faith, they are asked: "Who is your Lord and Savior?" They respond: "Jesus Christ is my Lord and Savior." There are no requirements that one be a certain race or gender or economic position in society. There are no requirements for a certain level of intelligence or sophistication or class or culture. No, simply faith. Faith alone—that is how we are saved; and that is the means by which we come into the body of believers. The visible church is the body of those who outwardly confess their faith in Jesus Christ.

Through the visible church God's mission and ministry take

shape in the world. The Confession of 1967 says that "to be reconciled to God is to be sent into the world as his reconciling community" (*BC* 9.31). The church is "entrusted with God's message of reconciliation" and witnesses to God's love and grace in Jesus Christ. The church is the "locus" or the place from which Christian ministry and mission emerge by the work of the Holy Spirit. We carry out the church's mission through the church's corporate witness to Christ in society. We minister in Christ's name by all that we do as individuals as disciples of our Master. To be part of the visible church is to commit oneself to witnessing to the Christian gospel of God's actions in Christ and to serving God with sisters and brothers of faith. This service is the church's ministry in the world as it seeks to be visible representatives of Jesus Christ. We are sustained and supported by God's Spirit, who equips the church and endows each believer with gifts for ministry.

The Invisible Church

Presbyterian theology has also recognized the "invisible church." The invisible church is the true church, which is known to God and to God alone. The invisible church is composed of those who are elected by God and have genuine faith in Jesus Christ. The distinction between visible and invisible church is important. A practical, pastoral problem is that often people will unite with a church and profess their faith but then fall away and not exercise their faith any further. Some may make an outward profession of faith that is not sincere or genuine. Some may join the church only as a matter of convenience, or to "look good," or to attain a certain status in the community. If our confession of faith in Jesus Christ is done for these reasons, then we are deceiving ourselves and others. But we can't deceive God. Ultimately, the invisible church is the true church of the elect, the true church of genuine believers. It is the church of all ages, what we call in the Apostles' Creed the "communion of saints." The invisible church is those who have truly professed their faith in Jesus Christ and who live out their commitment to Christ by the power of the Holy Spirit in their lives.

We must be very cautious in issuing judgments about other people and the genuineness of their faith. It is not up to us to decide who God should save. The doors of church membership are open for all those who desire to make a public profession of their faith in Jesus Christ. Whether or not their profession is genuine, or whether or not they will follow through by living a Christian life as a disciple of Jesus Christ, is not ours to judge or to prescribe. Only God knows for certain who truly believes. As Christians, we must be humble in considering ourselves—never, ever thinking of "boasting" about our faith. We cannot presume to assess others. We cannot judge them. As soon as we begin to boast or judge others with regard to their salvation, we cast doubt on the genuineness of our faith in the first place. Jesus warned, "Do not judge, so that you may not be judged" (Matt. 7:1). It is God alone who knows the heart (1 Sam. 16:7; Ps. 44:21; Acts 15:8).

The invisible church is known only to God. It is comprised of both the living and the dead. The true believers in Christ through all ages—past, present, and future—make up the invisible church. All the saints of old, from biblical times through the early church, the Middle Ages, during the days of the Reformation, and ever since are members of the invisible church. They have gone before us as believers in Jesus Christ. The church of tomorrow—all those who will come after us, our children and grandchildren, and millions yet unborn—comprise the invisible church as well. They will come after us as believers in Jesus Christ. This is the fullness of the "communion of saints." Presbyterian Christians have a "comprehensive view" of the church. The elect of every age, whose identity is known only to God, are the true and full church.

Characteristics of the Church

Christians are members of the "visible church"—the outward church—and the "invisible church"—the elect of God through all ages. Where is the church to be found, we ask? Where do we discover the church? Calvin and the Presbyterian tradition have typically answered this by saying that the church exists where the Word of God is preached and where the sacraments are rightly

administered (see *Institutes* 4.1.9). In some theological defini-
tions, a third characteristic, or mark of the church, is added: where
discipline is maintained (*BC* 3.18). The discipline of the church
is the way the church orders its life in obedience to God's Word
and to carry out its ministry.
These characteristics point us
to some important activities
of the church, particularly its
preaching and the sacraments.

> Christians are members of
> the "visible church"—the
> outward church—and the
> "invisible church"—the elect
> of God through all ages.

Preaching. One characteristic of the church in Presbyterian theology is that the
church exists where the Word
of God is preached. Presbyterian Christians have always had a
very high view of preaching. This means we consider the action of
preaching to be tremendously significant. Preaching is important
because it is a means God uses to spread the message of the gospel,
the message of Jesus Christ. Paul wrote that "faith comes from
what is heard, and what is heard comes through the word of Christ"
(Rom. 10:17). In preaching, Jesus Christ is made present to hearers. What more important event can you imagine? Preaching is a
gift of God, because through this human activity a divine action
occurs. In preaching, Jesus Christ becomes known and present.
The reality of Jesus Christ is conveyed. So highly do we regard the
importance of preaching that one confession, the Second Helvetic
Confession, written in 1566, says: "The Preaching of the Word of
God is the Word of God" (*BC* 5.004). Preaching is a form of God's
Word. Preaching is proclamation of the Word of God—meaning
the proclamation of Jesus Christ as he is known through the Scriptures, which are God's Word as well. The theologian Karl Barth
referred to the threefold form of the Word of God. There is the
incarnate Word, who is Jesus Christ. There is the *written* Word,
which is the Holy Scriptures. There is the *proclaimed* Word, which
is the preaching of Jesus Christ. All three forms are interrelated.
The living or incarnate Word, Jesus Christ, is known to us through
the Scriptures and through preaching. The written Word, the Scriptures, bear witness to the incarnate Word, Jesus Christ, who is

made present through preaching. The preached Word witnesses to the incarnate Word, Jesus Christ, and is based on the written Word, the Holy Scriptures. So preaching is a highly important action. We believe that as the Scriptures are proclaimed, God's presence and power become real to the hearers by the work of the Holy Spirit. Jesus Christ becomes known.

This means lives can be changed through preaching. Faith can begin, faith can grow and be nourished. No sermon can accomplish these effects all by itself. It is the Holy Spirit, who awakens faith and who through the preached Word causes faith to begin, or grow, or be nourished. So, on one hand, preaching is the most awesome of tasks. It is awesome because it is a divine activity. Through preaching a whole revolution in human life can occur. On the other hand, preaching is a very human activity, because sermons have to be conceived and written and delivered by preachers. None of this can be done perfectly from a human point of view. Every preacher preaches with a keen sense of his or her own human limitations. But the good news is that God uses human efforts, even when they fall far short of all that they can or should be, to convey the truth of the message of Jesus Christ. The divine works through the human. In preaching, the divine voice of God can be heard through the human words of the preacher.

> Lives can be changed through preaching. Faith can begin, faith can grow and be nourished.

Sacraments. A second characteristic of the church is that the church exists where the sacraments are rightly administered. The church is where Christian faith begins, is nourished, and grows. Faith begins in the church through God's Spirit, who draws people together—the people whom God has called or elected to be the body of Christ, the new people of God, the fellowship of believers in this world. As a sign of this faith, God has instituted two sacraments in the church. These two sacraments are means by which our faith is nourished.

Presbyterians in the Reformed tradition recognize the two sacraments of baptism and the Lord's Supper. Sacraments are special. Sacraments are gifts God gives to strengthen and nourish our faith.

They are outward or visible signs of a reality that is invisible. Through the sacraments, the benefits of the gospel are given to us. This is why we call sacraments "means of grace." God uses them to convey the grace of God to us.

Two images of a sacrament have been used to describe sacraments in the Presbyterian tradition. Sacraments are signs and seals.

1. *Sacraments are signs.* In the sacraments we see the gospel of Jesus Christ right before our eyes. In baptism, we see the water that represents the cleansing of our sin and the new life of faith in Christ. In the Lord's Supper, we see the bread and wine, which are Christ's body and blood given as a sacrifice for our sins so that we might have forgiveness, reconciliation, and new life. The outward elements of the sacraments—the water, the bread, and the wine—are signs of God's love, grace, and desire to bring us into a deeper relationship with God. When we participate in the sacraments, we give a sign to the whole watching world. We are aligning ourselves with the gospel of Jesus Christ. We are saying to all: We belong to Christ. We are witnessing to our faith in him. By participating in the sacraments we are wearing a badge of faith; we are a sign of our faith to the whole world.

> Sacraments are gifts God gives to strengthen and nourish our faith. They are outward or visible signs of a reality that is invisible.

2. *Sacraments are seals.* The image here is an old one. In ancient times, a document from the king, in order to be official and thus legal, had to have the king's seal on it. Sometimes the seal consisted of a wax pressing of the king's ring. When the document was thus sealed, it was official and carried with it all the king's authority and power. In the same way, as we participate in the sacraments, we receive through these actions the power and authority of God in our lives. The gospel of Jesus Christ is sealed in our lives by faith, which is the way we receive the sacraments. When we believe in the gospel, the benefits of the gospel are sealed within our hearts by the work of the Holy Spirit. What Jesus Christ has done for the world is received by me as being done *for* me.

Our faith is nourished and strengthened by receiving the benefits of Christ.

Baptism. Baptism is celebrated as a sacrament in the context of a worship service in the church. When baptism is administered, the Word of God is preached, faith is present, and the Holy Spirit is operative to apply the gospel to the one who is baptized. In baptism, sin is acknowledged, cleansing occurs through Christ, a union of the believer with Christ is established, and the gift of the Holy Spirit is given. Baptism is a sign of God's covenant. In that sense, it replaces circumcision as a mark of persons who are part of God's covenant community (Col. 2:11–12). In baptism, the Holy Spirit nourishes believers and makes the gospel effective in their lives in the covenant community.

Baptism is our entrance into Christ's church. Presbyterians in the Reformed tradition share the common Christian practice of baptizing infants. Infant baptism has been an important part of our heritage. When we baptize babies, we do so in the presence of the baby's parents or those who have parental roles and the worshiping congregation. In baptism, the parents act on behalf of the child in confessing their faith in Jesus Christ. They also promise to raise their child to hear and know the Christian gospel and to be a disciple of Jesus Christ ("in the nurture and admonition of the Lord," as older language put it). The parents present their child as part of the covenant community, believing that the promises of the gospel are for them and for their children (Acts 2:39). The covenant community also participates in the baptismal service. The congregation promises to take responsibilities as well. The people of the church promise to provide for the Christian nurture of the new member of the covenant community. This commits the church congregation to care for the child, to provide opportunities for education and service in Christ, and to pray for the child as the young one grows in a life of faith. In baptism, infants are welcomed into the body of Christ as children of the covenant.

Infant baptism is also a marvelous reminder of God's grace. Each of us comes like that helpless baby before God, no matter what our age. God reaches out in gracious election to bring us into the covenant community, the church, to give us the gift of faith, and to make us God's people in Jesus Christ. It is God's action that saves us—just as in infant baptism it is the action of the child's parents or those who have parental roles to present the helpless child. We are saved solely by God's grace, just as the little infant is brought into the believing community by the gracious action of parents. We do not baptize ourselves. Baptism is an act of the church administered *to* us. Infant baptism reminds us of God's initiative in our salvation.

> Infant baptism is also a marvelous reminder of God's grace. Each of us comes like that helpless baby before God, no matter what our age.

Lord's Supper. Baptism brings us into the church, where faith begins. In the church, our faith is also nurtured. It is nurtured through another means of God's grace, the sacrament of the Lord's Supper. The Lord's Supper is also called the Eucharist, Holy Communion, or simply Communion. Each of these terms points to a distinctive aspect of the Supper. It is the action by which we in the church remember and have our faith nourished by the action of our Lord Jesus Christ himself. On the night he was betrayed, Jesus instituted what we came to call this sacramental action at his last supper with his disciples (Luke 22:14–23). He took bread and wine, broke the bread, and said of it: "This is my body, which is given for you." Of the wine Jesus said: "This cup that is poured out for you is the new covenant in my blood." Then Jesus instituted the practice of the Lord's Supper by saying that sharing in these actions of eating and drinking are ways of remembering him and that by sharing in these actions we are proclaiming the Lord's death until he comes (1 Cor. 11:26).

The Lord's Supper is a gracious action given by Jesus Christ to nourish our Christian faith. Jesus used the common stuff of life—bread and wine—as means to strengthen our faith. As we eat and drink, in the context of the church community and the preaching of the Word of God, we are nourished in our faith because we receive the benefits of Christ's death on our behalf. All that Christ's life, death, and resurrection mean as actions of God are made real and effective for us by the power of the Holy Spirit as we eat and drink in the Supper. We receive the benefits of the salvation Christ has accomplished.

Jesus Christ is present in our service of Holy Communion. As we eat and drink the elements, we do so by faith. Through faith, we believe that these elements are means God uses to bring the benefits of Christ's death directly to us by the power of the Holy Spirit. This is a "spiritual" eating and drinking that we receive as we trust in Christ's promises and actions. As we do, our faith is nourished. God conveys the good news of the gospel to us through our senses—by hearing, seeing, tasting, smelling, and touching. All these are parts of the sacrament of the

> The Lord's Supper is a gracious action instituted by Jesus Christ to nourish our Christian faith. Jesus used the common stuff of life—bread and wine—as means to strengthen our faith.

Eucharist. When we see the elements on the Communion table, the words of the Gospel should ring in our ears. The Eucharist is much more than a mere "remembering," simply recalling some distant event. By the Holy Spirit, the power of Christ's life, death, and resurrection become ours in the sacrament through faith as we eat and drink. In the midst of a faithless world, we remember that there was one who was faithful to God, even Jesus Christ. In eating and drinking in the sacrament, we receive the benefits of what he has done for us in granting us salvation, forgiving our sins, and reconciling us with God and with others.

This is why we "celebrate" the Lord's Supper. Eating and drinking in the covenant community is a joyful action, full of praise and thanksgiving. Can you imagine any more wonderful event than receiving the benefits of the salvation provided by Jesus Christ in visible, tangible ways? We are properly sorry for our sins, for all our offenses against God. We remember the agony of Jesus' crucifixion, knowing that as he hung on the cross he hung there with the weight of our sin and the sin of the whole world on him. When we look at the cross we say, "God loves like that!" In these senses, we approach the Supper with reverence and awe. Yet in the Eucharist we also express unbounded joy and thanksgiving for the deep and unfathomable love that the cross of Christ reveals. We celebrate with reverence, awe, gratitude, and rejoicing. The Lord's Supper makes the benefits of Christ's sacrificial death and victorious resurrection real to us. This is the cause of our deepest rejoicing. The hymn writer exclaimed of the cross of Christ: "Love so amazing, so divine, demands my soul, my life, my all." As we eat and drink in the Eucharist, we are acknowledging the amazing love of God in Christ, and we are committing ourselves to live as Christ's servants and disciples, serving him and others according to the will of God by the power of the Holy Spirit within us and among us in the church.

Questions for Discussion

1. Why is the concept of "covenant" important for Presbyterians in understanding the church?
2. In what ways is it helpful to recognize that the church is both "visible" and "invisible"?
3. Have there been instances when preaching has been of special importance for your Christian life?
4. Why are the sacraments important to you?
5. Do you believe that a person has to be a member of the church to be a genuine Christian? Why, or why not?

12

Christian Life

In the church, our faith begins, is nourished, and grows. The growth of our life in the Christian faith is what theologians call "sanctification." Sanctification means "growth in holiness." It means our pilgrimage, our journey, our maturing in Christian faith. It is the process that begins after we receive salvation, in which we learn more and more of Christ and of God's will. It is our commitment to following God's will by living lives of service to God in the church and in the world as disciples of Jesus Christ. Sanctification means the development of our spiritual character, the nature of who we are as Christians.

We grow in faith, love, mercy, peace, joy, justice, and all the attitudes and ways of living God wants for us. We are to grow into conformity with the image of Jesus Christ (Eph. 4:15; 2 Pet. 3:18). In sanctification, our whole nature is being renewed by the power of the Holy Spirit. We seek, with the new wills given to us in salvation, to follow Jesus Christ, to live out God's will—rather than to live lives focused on ourselves and our own self-interests.

> Sanctification means the development of our spiritual character, the nature of who we are as Christians.

Growing in Faith

We recognize that our growth in faith takes place through the work of God's Holy Spirit within us. Yet God's Spirit does not work apart from our own human efforts. The Christian life is the work of God's Spirit within us and among us. But it takes shape in the context of our own actions. We pray, read the Scriptures, worship, and participate in the life and mission of the church. We do the things we believe God wants us to do. As we do those things, we sense God's power is at work within us, helping our faith grow and our lives in Christ take on ever-new dimensions of meaning.

Presbyterians have been big on sanctification. We believe God works through the processes of our lives to enable us to grow in grace, faith, and service. We establish educational institutions for the development of the mind. We establish hospitals to bring health and healing to the body. We establish churches for the worship of God. In those churches we establish Christian education and invest ourselves in the church's mission and ministry, so our faith will grow intellectually and through our actions. God does not want to "save us and forget us." God saves us to equip us for ministry and mission in this world. God gives us the resources to live our faith daily in all we do.

Worship. One way that this equipping takes place for us is through worship. Worship is absolutely crucial for our Christian existence, just as it was for Israel in the Old Testament. We worship God regularly, weekly, as we gather with other believers in church as the fellowship of faith. Participating in worship in the church is not an option for us as Christians; it's a basic necessity. We gather in the covenant community for praise, petition, and thankfulness for who God is and what God has done.

We also worship God daily as we use the means of grace God gives us—reading the Scriptures and praying to God. We worship as Christians and give our full attention to the God who is our creator, who redeems us in Jesus Christ, and who is present with us by the Holy Spirit. In worship we praise God, thank God, pray to God, and listen to God. Worship enables us to speak to God and to hear God speaking to us in the context of the Christian community. Worship provides the orientation for our Christian lives. As we praise God, seek God, wrestle with what we believe God is calling us to be and to do, worship is the setting in which our quest to live the Christian life takes place.

Prayer. Presbyterians believe mightily in prayer. Calvin called prayer "the chief exercise of faith, and by which we daily receive God's benefits" (*Institutes* 3.20.1). Most simply, prayer is conversation with God (*Institutes* 3.20.4).

Why pray? We pray not only because God commands us but also because we believe God hears and answers our prayers (Jer. 29:12). This is the way the psalmist addressed God: "O you who answer prayer!" (Ps. 65:2). God commands us to pray in the "day of trouble" (Ps. 50:15). Jesus says "to pray always and not to lose heart" (Luke 18:1). Paul says we are to "pray without ceasing" (1 Thess. 5:17). Prayer is motivated by our love and gratitude to God. It arises out of our lives daily and becomes part of the rhythm of our Christian existence. Prayer is expressing our thoughts, desires, and praise to God, as well as "listening" in quietness for God's Spirit to speak to us and within us. As we enter into prayer, we "pray in the Spirit" (Eph. 6:18). The Holy Spirit helps us pray, even as we stammer in our weakness. Who of us really knows how to pray "as we ought"—as we should? We don't. But God

> Prayer is expressing our thoughts, desires, and praise to God, as well as "listening" in quietness for God's Spirit to speak to us and within us.

graciously gives the Spirit to us to intercede for us "with sighs too deep for words" (Rom. 8:26). What a blessing!

Often prayers are described as having four parts. Our prayers in public worship with the Christian community as well as our individual, private prayers gather round these four elements. First is *Adoration*, where we praise God for who God is and focus our attention on the greatness of the triune God. Second is *Confession*, in which we admit our sinfulness and specify those things we have done, or have failed to do, that have caused us not to live up to the image of God and God's will within us. Third is *Thanksgiving*. Here we thank God for all our blessings, for all God's acts, and for all God has done. Finally, there is *Supplication*, in which we let our "requests be made known to God" (Phil. 4:6) as we pray for the world, for others, and for ourselves. Taken together, the first letters of these four parts spell ACTS. Prayer is speaking and listening that leads to action and activity on our parts, to enact that for which we have prayed or that which God lays upon our hearts to do.

God answers prayer. We marvel at the many ways this can occur. But one main way that God answers is through the actions of ourselves and others. We are the means God uses to answer prayer—for others, and at times for ourselves. God uses other people to *be* the answers to our prayers as well. So prayer is not a kind of automatic "cruise control" for the Christian life—a ritual in which to be engaged so that we may "coast along" the highway of life. Instead, it is a very comforting and challenging activity that brings us into the presence of God and then leads us onward, by the Spirit, into the ways and paths God would have us follow. One never knows when one begins to pray just where that prayer will lead, to whom it will lead, or into what new directions our lives may be turned. So prayer in this sense is "dangerous"! Our whole lives may be radically changed when we pray! Prayer is our lifeline in the Christian faith. Presbyterians pray to experience God in our midst and in our hearts. We pray to seek God's will and find our ways on our journeys of faith.

Law of God. How do we know what to do and what path to take? How do we know the kind of Christian lives God wants us to live? Presbyterians have always believed that one place to look is at the law of God. Presbyterian Christians have stressed that the law of God, which we find in the Ten Commandments (Ex. 20:1–17), is a good gift from God. God gave the Law to the people of Israel as an expression of God's will. God communicates the way life is to be lived as a covenant community through the Ten Commandments. The divine intention for human society is conveyed through the prescriptions that God gives. The magnificent Psalm 119 is the longest chapter in the Bible. Nearly every verse makes reference to God's law, precepts, commandments, decrees, or ordinances—all expressions of the divine will. The psalmist proclaims, "Truly I love your commandments more than gold, more than fine gold. Truly I direct my steps by all your precepts; I hate every false way" (Ps. 119:127–28). Those who "walk in the law of the LORD" are "happy" (Ps. 119:1).

For Christians who have been saved by God's love in Jesus Christ and drawn together in the church by the work of the Holy Spirit, the law of God in the Ten Commandments is still intensely important. Now, as Christians, we turn to the law of God to see how God wants us to live. We seek to know God's will

> We do not obey the law of God to make ourselves look good or upright in our communities. As Christians we obey the law of God out of gratitude for what God has done for us in Jesus Christ.

for our lives as Christians, and the law of God is one place where that will is still conveyed. Now, as Christians, we seek to obey God's law. We do so not in order to gain righteousness in God's sight. We could never accomplish that! We do not obey God's law in order to be saved or receive salvation. None of us could ever be perfectly obedient to God's will as expressed in God's law. We do not obey the law of God to make ourselves look good or upright in our communities. As Christians we obey the law of God out of gratitude for what God has done for us in Jesus Christ. We obey the law and follow the commandments as a way to express our thanksgiving to God. We obey God's law as a response to God's love in Jesus Christ. We do what God wants us to do as our way of saying "thank you" to God for the gracious gift of salvation. So we see God's law as God's good gift to us. The law of God shows us what kind of behavior God wants us to avoid. God shows us the kind of behavior that will ruin our lives and our relationships with God and others. Yet, positively, we are free to do anything else in all the world—except what the law forbids. If we live our lives in this way, we will find the freedom and the joy that God promises. Calvin believed that the main purpose of the law of God was to show believers how to live (*Institutes* 2.7.12). We can say with the psalmist: "How I love your law!" and "I find my delight in your commandments, because I love them" (Pss. 47, 119:97). So the law of God as a positive, useful guide for the Christian life has been an important emphasis of our Presbyterian heritage.

Our sanctification, or growth in faith, is a process that is not completed this side of death. In some forms of the Wesleyan or Methodist tradition, there is the doctrine of perfection. The view is that some Christians may become so totally "sanctified," or purified in their faith, that they attain a perfection of love. They will be able to obey God's law and to love as fully and completely as God wants and thus avoid sin and offenses to God and to neighbors. We Presbyterian Christians are not so optimistic. We see the Christian life as a kind of zigzag pattern: we grow in our faith, we may have setbacks, but we keep on moving. It's a kind of spiral, around and around but also moving up and ahead. Yet we never attain an ultimate goal in this life. We never come to the place where we have fully and finally "arrived" as Christians or attained the ultimate perfection where we can be all that we can be, as we might hope. This perfection will occur—in heaven, after death, but not before. God is never finished with us as long as we live. It's like those signs on

> Presbyterian Christians believe we are always "under construction." We are never "finished" with God in the sense of attaining the fullness of the Christian life that God would ultimately desire.

highways to show that maintenance work is being done on the road: "Under Construction." Presbyterian Christians believe we are always "under construction." We are never "finished" with God in the sense of attaining the fullness of the Christian life that God would ultimately desire. We continue to serve God, follow Christ, respond to the Holy Spirit, day in and day out— faithfully and with commitment, over years and years of service in the church, believing that God's work in our lives is always continuing. God is never "finished" with us! We believe that God's Spirit is at work within us, both to will and to work in ways beyond our knowing. God is the one who is at work within us, accomplishing "abundantly far more than all we can ask or imagine" (Eph. 3:20).

Calling. We keep on keeping on in the Christian life, because as Presbyterians we believe that God has called us. God has called us to be followers of Jesus Christ; and God has called us to live out our calling, or our vocation, in the context of this world. We are called to service. We are called to mission and ministry in the church and in the world. Our vocations are sometimes referred to as our "jobs." We believe that we as Christians can, and indeed do, live out our callings to be servants of Christ in the daily work we do. As we serve others, we serve Christ. As we use the gifts God has given us for the common good of our neighbors and society, we are living as God desires us to live.

We live out our vocations in terms of our jobs. But even more, our vocations are who we are. We follow our callings as disciples of Jesus Christ in whatever work we do—and we live out that calling as Christians. We have a sense that who we are is what really counts. Who we are goes with us wherever we go, in whatever work or occupation or job in which we find ourselves. This is what gives us a lively sense of God's presence and power. We realize that God is working through us—*through* us!—God is working through us as we work at the occupations or jobs we have. God works through all the relationships we establish. When Presbyterians take this view of vocation seriously, realizing God's presence and power at work within us every day, we experience renewal in our churches. God's Spirit enables us to sense the excitement of seeing what God is doing and how God is working in our lives, providentially, in the common experiences we have every day. As we serve, in ministry and mission, we will see what God is doing through us, through the likes of "people like us." This is exciting! Our Christian vocation is both who we are and what we do. When we see our whole lives from that perspective—that we are serving God in everything—then our lives take on great meaning and exhilaration. We Presbyterians take as our life's goal what Paul prescribed to the Corinthians: "Whatever you do, do

> We live out our vocations in terms of our jobs. But even more, our vocations are who we are. We follow our callings as disciples of Jesus Christ in whatever work we do—and we live out that calling as Christians.

everything for the glory of God" (1 Cor. 10:31). This is the goal of our Christian lives.

Questions for Discussion

1. In what ways do you recognize yourself as growing in faith?
2. In what ways is worship important to you?
3. Have you had experiences in which you are sure that God has answered your prayers?
4. In what ways is the law of God helpful in your Christian life?
5. Are you aware of living out your "calling" or "vocation" in daily life? In what ways?

13

The Future Life

We all wonder about the future. Not a day goes past that we do not think, in some regard, about what lies ahead. Most of the time this is on the common level: What is on my calendar for the week? When do I have to do grocery shopping? What is the school schedule for my children?

Yet at times we reflect on an even bigger picture. We wonder about the future of the world and about our personal destinies. Will the world go on indefinitely? Is there an end to history? What is eternity? What lies ahead after death? These questions propel us into the realm of God's future work, both in this world and in the next. Theologians call this dimension of theology "eschatology," meaning the study of the "last things" or "end things." It refers both to God's ultimate plan and purposes for the end of history and beyond as well as to issues of our eternal life, our life after death.

The Big Picture: God's Reign

The Bible is the story of salvation. It tells us of God's work in this world to call a people who will love and serve throughout the world. The Bible also gives us a "big picture" of what God is doing in human history, in and through both the covenant people of God and in all peoples and cultures. The work of God in history is to establish God's kingdom, or God's reign.

> The work of God in history is to establish God's kingdom, or God's reign.

The Old Testament people of God, Israel, worshiped God as their king. The Psalms are full of "kingship" language, acknowledging the role that the God of Israel played in the nation's life. The people worshiped their sovereign: "Sing praises to God, sing praises; sing praises to our King, sing praises. For God is the king of all the earth; sing praises with a psalm. God is king over the nations; God sits on his holy throne" (Ps. 47:6–8). God rules all nations, including Israel, and God is also the personal "king" of faithful Israelites: "Yet God my King is from of old, working salvation in the earth" (Ps. 74:12).

God's work in the nation has direction and purpose. The divine purpose is to establish God's ultimate reign throughout all the earth. This reign will be marked by the characteristics of God that ancient Israel had come to know in its history—righteousness, mercy, justice, peace. This was the social vision of the Hebrew prophets, who looked forward in anticipation to God's future as the time when all nations and all peoples would acknowledge God's sovereignty and rule (Isa. 2:2–4). The prophet Isaiah proclaimed: "How beautiful upon the mountains are the feet of the messenger who announces peace, who brings good news, who announces salvation, who says to Zion, 'Your God reigns'" (Isa. 52:7). This is the image made famous in the prophet Micah:

And many nations shall come and say:
"Come, let us go up to the mountain of the LORD,
    to the house of the God of Jacob;
that he may teach us his ways
    and that we may walk in his paths."
For out of Zion shall go forth instruction,
    and the word of the LORD from Jerusalem.
He shall judge between many peoples,
    and shall arbitrate between strong nations far away;
they shall beat their swords into plowshares,
    and their spears into pruning hooks;
nation shall not lift up sword against nation,
    neither shall they learn war any more;

but they shall all sit under their own vines and under their own fig
    trees,
and no one shall make them afraid;
for the mouth of the LORD of hosts has spoken.

                                      (Mic. 4:2–4)

This ultimate reign of God is marked by the knowledge of God,
obedience to God and God's just rule, and the peace (Heb. *shalom*)
among nations. This is the direct action of God.

    This is also the "kingdom of God" about which Jesus taught in
his many parables. He likens the "kingdom of heaven" to common incidents or experiences (see the parables in Matthew 13).
Through this teaching tool, Jesus transformed the consciousness
of his hearers, to teach them some important aspects of who God
is and how God desires people to live in this world. Most scholars
agree that the central theme of Jesus' whole message is the coming of the kingdom of God. Jesus began his ministry "proclaiming
the good news [gospel] of God, and saying, 'The time is fulfilled,
and the kingdom of God has come near; repent, and believe in
the good news'" (Mark 1:14–15; Matt. 4:12–17). Jesus saw his
own ministry as inaugurating God's reign among the people, as a
fulfillment of God's promises to "proclaim release to the captives
and recovery of sight to the blind, to let the oppressed go free, to
proclaim the year of the Lord's favor" (Luke 4:18–19, citing Isa.
61:1–2). Jesus' mission emerged from this understanding. He said,
"I must proclaim the good news of the kingdom of God to the other
cities also; for I was sent for
this purpose" (Luke 4:43).

    So God's reign is taking
shape in this world. It is at
work imperceptibly, from
small beginnings, but its suc-
cess is assured (see Matt.
13:31–33). The early Chris-
tian church believed the future of God's ultimate reign was
assured because of the resurrection of Jesus Christ from the dead.
The resurrection is the pivot of history. God's raising Jesus from

> God's reign is taking shape in
> this world. It is at work imper-
> ceptibly, from small begin-
> nings, but its success is assured.

the dead is the assurance that the future resurrection of believers will occur. Believers who are united with Christ through his death will share also in resurrection glory. As Paul put it, "If we have been united with him in a death like his, we will certainly be united with him in a resurrection like his" (Rom. 6:5). Christ's resurrection is the assurance of our own resurrection and eternal life (see 1 Cor. 15:12–28). Christ will ultimately hand over his kingdom "to God the Father, after he has destroyed every ruler and every authority and power. For he must reign until he has put all his enemies under his feet. The last enemy to be destroyed is death" (1 Cor. 15:24–26). This means that the establishment of God's eternal reign has already begun. In the resurrection of Jesus Christ we have a preview of its final fulfillment and accomplishment. All powers and oppositions to God will ultimately be crushed. The Confession of 1967 says that "the kingdom represents the triumph of God over all that resists his will and disrupts his creation" (*BC* 9.54). The petitions in the Lord's Prayer are answered: God's kingdom *will* come and God's will *will* be done (Matt. 6:10). The vision of the book of Revelation will come true: "Hallelujah! For the Lord our God the Almighty reigns" (Rev. 19:6).

> . . . the establishment of God's eternal reign has already begun. In the resurrection of Jesus Christ we have a preview of its final fulfillment and accomplishment.

We live as Christians, seeking God's will, seeking to serve God in all we do, because ultimately we believe God's purposes will be carried out. The will of God will finally prevail in this world. Presbyterians have an "optimistic" view of the future. Yet our optimism is not based on human aspirations or accomplishments. If our view of the future rested solely on the human, then surely pessimism would reign! Instead, we hope in God. We trust in God. We believe the God who started it all will complete it all. We believe that the God who creates and redeems is also the God who reigns eternally, in the future kingdom of God. We believe this is the God who saves us and who judges us in Jesus Christ and whose reign will have no end.

All God's purposes will come to pass. In the end God's will overcomes all. We look forward to the new heavens and new earth, where God's kingdom and reign will be fully realized, forever.

God's reign is taking shape in the world. It is not clear and perceptible to human senses. Jesus told his parables for anyone with ears to listen (Mark 4:9; Luke 8:8). So we must look and listen to all around us in order to see where God's reign is breaking into our world here and now. We see God's reign happening when the values that Jesus proclaimed and lived are embodied and established in people and places around us. When love is shared, care is given, justice administered, reconciliation accomplished, or peace prevails—God's reign is at work. God's kingdom does not take shape in a clearly evolutionary pattern in history. We cannot assume that more aspects of the twenty-first century are congruent with the reign of God than were in the fifteenth century or the fourth century. We have learned not to trust the little motto "Every day, in every way, we are getting better." The amount of human-inflicted death through war in the twentieth century, for example, makes it impossible to believe that every century of human history is necessarily an improvement on the one that has gone before, in terms of movement toward God's reign. Human "progress" can never be equated with God's kingdom.

> God's kingdom in all its fullness will break into history at the time God chooses.

Instead, God's kingdom, in all its fullness, will break into history at the time God chooses. We live now, after the resurrection of Jesus Christ, as members of the church who know the reality of God's kingdom in Jesus Christ himself. Early Christians said the kingdom was *autobaselia*, a Greek word meaning a "self-kingdom." By that they meant that the kingdom of God has already come in the person of Jesus Christ. We can watch for those aspects of God's reign that show up in our own experience every day. But this is not the complete story. The church anticipates God's coming, final kingdom when, as the Scriptures say,

> at the name of Jesus
>   every knee should bend,
>   in heaven and on earth and under the earth,
>   and every tongue should confess
>   that Jesus Christ is Lord,
>   to the glory of God the Father.
>
> (Phil. 2:10–11)

We look forward to the glorious coming of God's reign in its eternal fullness. Sometimes we say we live in an "already, but not yet" mode. God's kingdom has "already" come—in Jesus Christ. Yet as we pray in the Lord's Prayer, "Thy kingdom come," we also anticipate the final manifestation of God's reign, a manifestation that has "not yet" come to completion.

The Future

It is natural to wonder when all this will take place. Is the coming kingdom of God near, or will it still be thousands of years in the future? Presbyterians answer: We don't know. We don't know because the Bible does not give us clear or unambiguous answers about exactly how the future will take shape.

There are parts of the Bible that are written to affirm certain aspects of the future. Sections of the Bible are called "apocalyptic literature." They speak about the end of the world and human history. They are written in highly symbolic language. They predict great cataclysms or disasters, wars and battles. But their message is that God will triumph over all the forces of evil. In the Old Testament, apocalyptic literature is found in the books of Daniel and Ezekiel. In the New Testament, the book of Revelation is in this genre. Apocalyptic literature is usually written by people who are being persecuted in order to maintain their hope in the triumph of their cause. Apocalyptic literature in the Christian Scriptures also conveys Christian hope. It describes very graphically the ultimate conquest of evil and all that opposes God, while proclaiming the final victory of God over all that resists and combats the divine will. The symbolic images in the book of Revelation and magnificent visions such as the new Jerusalem (Rev. 21:9–27), the "river of the water of life" (Rev. 22), and "a new heaven and a new earth" (Rev. 21:1) unmistakably affirm belief in God's ultimate triumph, victory, and reign over all.

The images and scenarios of apocalyptic literature are not intended to be interpreted literally. They are ways of trying to express great truths in symbolic language. Apocalyptic literature is powerful because it tries to express the inexpressible and to communicate a tremendous message of truth that goes beyond what can be captured in a simple series of literal statements.

> The images and scenarios of apocalyptic literature are not intended to be interpreted literally. They are ways of trying to express great truths in symbolic language.

So, then, we need to recognize that as we try to interpret much of what the Bible says about the future, we should seek the theological truths being conveyed rather than focus on a literal anticipation of events or happenings. The Bible's language about the future is powerful and true language. But its truth is in the realities it conveys, not in attempts to interpret each event or image literally.

The Bible does not give us a detailed chronology of future events on the divine timetable. A large number of popular religious books deal with the future, Bible prophecy, or the end of the world. These all affirm that they are based on the Scriptures. But as we examine them on the bookshelves, we find they all predict a different scenario of events or a different sequence of happenings between now and the final kingdom of God. This should be enough to make us wary of all such attempts to construct a biblical blueprint for the future!

There are some elements, however, that are clearly parts of the biblical affirmations about the future.

The Second Coming of Christ. The Apostles' Creed affirms that we believe Jesus will "come again." This promise is a "blessed hope" (Titus 2:13) and has been especially meaningful for those who are oppressed and persecuted. It has given them hope for the future, and it still does.

Jesus himself predicted his coming again (Matt. 24:30; Mark 13:24–27; John 14:3). The angels in the story of Jesus' ascension referred to it (Acts 1:11). The early church had a lively anticipation that Jesus would return and would return soon (Phil. 3:20; 1 Thess. 4:15). Throughout history, Christians have looked for "signs of the time," or events that they believe may be fulfillments of Bible prophecy or predictions that indicate the return of Christ is near.

Yet it is important to recognize that even Jesus did not know the time of his second coming. He said, "But about that day and hour no one knows, neither the angels of heaven, nor the Son, but only the Father" (Matt. 24:36). Presbyterians take this statement seriously, and so most do not try to look at history or current events and interpret these as fulfillments of biblical prophecy.

A better approach is this: We believe with certainty that Jesus Christ will come again. This is the event that will be the "end game," the beginning of the "end times." We recognize we cannot predict when this will be—it may be today, or tomorrow, or in four thousand years. So we should live as Jesus urged, with watchfulness (Mark 13:32–36) or expectancy. In other words, we can believe that the second coming of Jesus Christ is imminent, but not necessarily immediate. Jesus may return at any time (imminent). But Jesus' return may not be immediate—it may not happen for centuries to come. As we live, we should always be ready to find our physical lives ended with the return of Christ. But we invest our lives in our vocations and in service to Christ knowing that we may die before Christ comes again. So we live and serve in the now. At the same time, our prayer should always be: "Come, Lord Jesus!" (Rev. 22:20).

> We can believe that the second coming of Jesus Christ is imminent, but not necessarily immediate.

Last Judgment. The Apostles' Creed also affirms that we believe Jesus Christ will come again "to judge the quick [living] and the dead." Divine judgment is a reality throughout the Bible. In the Old Testament, God judges the earth and its peoples (Pss. 50:6; 82:8). Israel was judged by God for its unfaithfulness and sin (Ezek. 18:30; Jer. 4:12; 25:31). Jesus anticipates a day of judgment

(Matt. 10:15; 25:31–46; John 5:22), and judgment is a reality that all humans face because of their sin (Rom. 2:1–11; Heb. 9:27; 2 Pet. 2:9). Judgment may take place in this life (John 9:39), and even begins with the church—since the church as the covenant community knows God's will, but still sins (1 Pet. 4:17). The Bible speaks of a general resurrection, in which all who have died will be raised to face a future judgment (John 5:25–29; 1 Cor. 15:12–18; 1 Thess. 4:13–19). Paul said that "there will be a resurrection of both the righteous and the unrighteous" (Acts 24:15). So in the future, "All of us must appear before the judgment seat of Christ, so that each may receive recompense for what has been done in the body, whether good or evil" (2 Cor. 5:10).

Final States. The last judgment as portrayed in Scripture relates to ultimate destinies. Jesus' parable of the sheep and the goats in Matthew 25:31–46 contrasts "eternal punishment" with "eternal life" (v. 46). Traditionally, these two final destinations are referred to as "hell" and "heaven" (Matt. 10:28; Mark 9:43, 45; Luke 10:20; Phil. 3:20). Jesus Christ as judge (Matt. 25:31–32; John 5:27) will judge all persons according to their lives in relation to the will of God (Rom. 2:1–16). Images associated with hell are "furnace of fire" (Matt. 13:42); "lake of fire" (Rev. 20:14–15); and a place where the "worm never dies, and the fire is never quenched" (Mark 9:48). Images associated with heaven are those of a place (John 14:2) where the promise of "eternal life" (Matt. 19:29; John 6:40; 10:28; Rom. 6:23) is enjoyed by the saints in the eternal presence of God and the whole heavenly host (Rev. 21; 22).

Our Futures

Presbyterians believe God's reign is established, is being established, and will be established eternally, forever. We believe in Christ's second coming, judgment, and a final destiny. How do these biblical realities relate to our lives as Presbyterian Christians? What about our own futures?

Our Death. The event in our future that may seem most real to us as we anticipate the days ahead is our death. We know that we will die. Unless Jesus Christ returns to earth before the days of our lives on earth are finished, we will die.

Theologically, we believe our real "death" has already occurred. The death that matters most to us is our death to the power of sin and our new, resurrected life as believers in Christ. This was Paul's point when he wrote: "We know that our old self was crucified with him so that the body of sin might be destroyed, and we might no longer be enslaved to sin. For whoever has died is freed from sin. But if we have died with Christ, we believe that we will also live with him" (Rom. 6:6–8). Our life of faith, united with Jesus Christ, is the "new life"—the "eternal life" we share with Christ now and through eternity.

Yet our physical functionings will cease and we will die. Death is not an ultimate terror for the Christian. The answer to the first question of the Heidelberg Catechism puts things in perspective for us:

Q. 1. What is your only comfort in life and in death?

A. That I am not my own, but belong—body and soul, in life and in death—to my faithful Savior, Jesus Christ. He has fully paid for all my sins with his precious blood, and has set me free from the tyranny of the devil. He also watches over me in such a way that not a hair can fall from my head without the will of my Father in heaven; in fact, all things must work together for my salvation.

Because I belong to him, Christ, by his Holy Spirit, assures me of eternal life and makes me wholeheartedly willing and ready from now on to live for him. (*BC* 4.001)

Put succinctly, the Brief Statement of Faith begins by affirming that "in life and in death we belong to God" (*BC* 10.1). This is our ultimate assurance and security—to belong to God in Jesus Christ, held by the power of the Holy Spirit. In his resurrection, Jesus Christ has defeated the power of death as our "last enemy," which is destroyed (1 Cor. 15:26). While we naturally fear death as an unknown, death holds no ultimate terror because we are secure in God's electing and gracious love in Jesus Christ.

> This is our ultimate assurance and security—to belong to God in Jesus Christ, held by the power of the Holy Spirit.

Our Judgment. We are used

to seeing hideous pictures of "the last judgment," which display the horrors of eternal punishment, damnation, and condemnation. The verse from Hebrews rings in our ears: "It is a fearful thing to fall into the hands of the living God" (Heb. 10:31).

Yet for those who know Jesus Christ, even the last judgment holds no terror. For we remember that our judge, Jesus Christ, is also our Savior—the one who knows us best, loves us most. The Heidelberg Catechism says it well:

> Q. 52 How does Christ's return "to judge the living and the dead" comfort you?

> A. In all distress and persecution, with uplifted head, I confidently await the very judge who has already offered himself to the judgment of God in my place and removed the whole curse from me. (BC 4.052)

This is a word of comfort for us. Our judge has already been judged in our place. For us, Jesus Christ has died. Calvin caught the confidence of this reality when he wrote:

> Here arises a wonderful consolation: that we perceive judgment to be in the hands of him who has already destined us to share with him the honor of judging [Matt. 19:28]. . . . No mean assurance this—that we shall be brought before no other judgment seat than that of our Redeemer, to whom we must look for our salvation. (Institutes 2.16.18)

What greater assurance or comfort can we have! We face judgment from the one who has died to save us (Rom. 5:8).

Our Final State. We will be resurrected, we will come to judgment, and we will enter into the fullness of eternal life. Here is a glorious guarantee: "And this is what he has promised us, eternal life" (1 John 2:25). We receive resurrection bodies, new spiritual bodies that will be capable of enjoying the glories of eternal life (1 Cor. 15:35–49; cf. Phil. 3:21). This is a destiny to dream about! The Larger Catechism says of the righteous that they

> shall be received into heaven, where they shall be fully and forever freed from all sin and misery; filled with inconceivable joy; made perfectly holy and happy both in body and soul, in

the company of innumerable saints and angels, but especially in the immediate vision and fruition of God the Father, of our Lord Jesus Christ, and of the Holy Spirit, to all eternity. And this is the prefect and full communion, which the members of the invisible Church shall enjoy with Christ in glory, at the resurrection and day of judgment. (*BC* 7.200)

This vision of ultimate blessedness is beyond the power of words to capture. We believe in its coming reality because God is faithful and God has promised that through the resurrection of Jesus Christ, God "gives us the victory" (1 Cor. 15:57) of eternal life, both now and forever. Calvin said, "Christ rose again that he might have us as companions in the life to come" (*Institutes* 3.25.3). The magnificence of the "new heaven and the new earth" is our ultimate comfort and joy, where God will "wipe every tear from their eyes. Death will be no more; mourning and crying and pain will be no more, for the first things have passed away" (Rev. 21:4). Eternity will be spent in the everlasting praise of God. For the saints, "there will be no more night; they need no light or lamp or sun, for the Lord God will be their light, and they will reign forever and ever" (Rev. 22:5).

> "Christ rose again that he might have us as companions in the life to come."—John Calvin, *Institutes*

Questions for Discussion

1. What are examples of God's reign being established around us?
2. What are some implications of believing that the second coming of Jesus Christ is imminent but not necessarily immediate?
3. In what ways does our Christian faith help us face the experience of death?
4. Why does the "last judgment" not need to hold terror for Christians?
5. What do you think the experience of heaven will be like?

To the Glory of God!

*W*e have come a long way from the beginning. We have considered our Presbyterian beliefs and some of our distinctive emphases in "The God Who Reveals, Creates, and Guides"; "The Christ Who Saves People like Us"; and "The Church, Where Faith Begins, Is Nourished, and Grows." Through it all, our emphasis has been on the triune God and God's work in this world and among people, as Father, Son, and Holy Spirit. Presbyterians join with all other Christians in worship and praise to God for who God is and what God has done—and for what God is doing in our midst. As we seek to be faithful disciples of Jesus Christ—disciples who understand ourselves to be formed by our Presbyterian tradition—we have a rich theological reservoir on which to draw. We have the theological resources we need for our journeys of faith and service. As we all seek to understand our faith more fully, may we all give thanks to God for our wonderful heritage. May we seek always new insights, so that the church, which is reformed, may always also "be reformed" according to the will of God and Holy Scripture. May the Presbyterian heritage live in strength and vitality, seeking not our own glory, but always the glory of God!

Case Studies

By David Maxwell

1. A church friend goes to the Holy Land and is baptized in the Jordan River. Another church member, a high school student, reports being rebaptized at a retreat led by another church. Both claim that their first baptism really wasn't meaningful because they were baptized as infants and don't remember it. What do you think? What would you say to them?

2. A group of friends are discussing the Trinity. One thinks it is in the Bible but doesn't know where. Another says she doesn't see the point of this if there is only one God. How would you explain the Trinity?

3. In a casual conversation among friends from various religious beliefs, the word "predestination" comes up. Someone points at you and says, "You're the Presbyterian in the group. What do you think? Are we predestined to heaven or hell? Do we have no control over our destiny?" How would you reply?

4. A young person is explaining global climate change to your church group. Someone in the group says, "I believe that God is in total control of God's creation. We really can't do anything. It's God's will." How would you reply?

5. A group at church is discussing the importance of Jesus' death. Some say he had to die to pay for our sins, and we should be thankful. Some say he died because he took on the powers of evil, and we should follow his example. What do you think?

6. Your church receives a letter from a guest who attended worship last week. He is outraged that a big loaf of bread was used during communion and many crumbs dropped on the floor and were not picked up. He said it was like you left the body of Christ all over the place. What do you think? How would you reply?

7. You walk in on a heated discussion in a Sunday school class about the role of the church in politics. One side says the church has no business meddling in politics and discussing worldly affairs: "We should be preparing people for their salvation." Another side says the exact opposite: the church must be relevant and help its members participate faithfully in politics. What do you think?

8. A discussion arises about how the church is seen by others. Some say the church has been so hateful and judgmental of others that no one wants to come anymore. Others say the church has the responsibility to speak a moral voice to the world if the church is to be faithful. What do you think? Are the two positions necessarily exclusive to one another? Does the Bible or Presbyterian doctrines offer any guidelines?

9. A young couple comes to your church seeking baptism of their newborn baby girl, who is in the critical care unit of a local hospital. They tell you that it is very urgent because the baby might not live, and they don't want her to go to hell if she's not baptized. What would you say to the couple about the Presbyterian understanding of baptism? What would you do?

10. A middle-aged man comes to your church who has just served a five-year term in prison. He had worked in the financial investment business and was found guilty of stealing money from clients. Many elderly people in your community lost the little security they had and have suffered greatly due to the actions of this man. He now wants to join your church. What would you do? Why?

For Further Study

Angell, James W. *How to Spell Presbyterian*. Newly rev. ed. Louisville, KY: Geneva Press, 2002.

Being Reformed: Faith Seeking Understanding. Adult Curriculum. Congregational Ministries Publishing. Presbyterian Church (U.S.A). http://www.presbyterianmission.org/ministries/theology-formation -and-evangelism/curriculum/adult-curriculum/.

Calvin, John. *Institutes of the Christian Religion*. 2 vols. Library of Christian Classics. Ed. John T. McNeill. Trans. Ford Lewis Battles. Philadelphia: Westminster Press, 1960.

The Constitution of the Presbyterian Church (U.S.A). Part I, Book of Confessions. Louisville, KY: Office of the General Assembly, Presbyterian Church (U.S.A.), 2016.

Gerstner, John H. *Theology for Everyman*. Chicago: Moody Press, 1965.

Guthrie, Shirley C. *Always Being Reformed: Faith for a Fragmented World*. Louisville, KY: Westminster John Knox Press, 1996.

———. *Christian Doctrine*. Rev. ed. Louisville, Ky.: Westminster John Knox Press, 1994.

Johnson, Earl S., Jr. *Witness without Parallel: Eight Biblical Texts That Make Us Presbyterian*. Louisville, KY: Geneva Press, 2003.

Leitch, Addison H. *A Layman's Guide to Presbyterian Beliefs*. Grand Rapids, MI: Zondervan Publishing House, 1967.

Leith, John H. *Introduction to the Reformed Tradition: A Way of Being the Christian Community*. Atlanta: John Knox Press, 1980.

Lingle, Walter L., and John W. Kuykendall. *Presbyterians: Their History and Beliefs*. Atlanta: John Knox Press, 1978.

McKim, Donald K., ed. *Calvin's Institutes: Abridged Edition*. Louisville, KY: Westminster John Knox Press, 2000.

———. *The Church: Presbyterian Perspectives*. Eugene, OR: Wipf & Stock, 2017.

———. *Introducing the Reformed Faith*. Louisville, KY: Westminster John Knox Press, 2001.

———. *More Presbyterian Questions, More Presbyterian Answers*. Revised. Louisville, KY: Westminster John Knox Press, 2017.

———. *Presbyterian Faith That Lives Today*. Louisville, KY: Geneva Press, 2014.

———. *Presbyterian Questions, Presbyterian Answers*. Revised. Louisville, KY: Westminster John Knox Press, 2017.

———, ed. *The Westminster Handbook to Reformed Theology*. Louisville, KY: Westminster John Knox Press, 2001.

Plunkett, Stephen W. *This We Believe: Eight Truths Presbyterians Affirm*. Louisville, KY: Geneva Press, 2002.

Rogers, Jack. *Presbyterian Creeds: A Guide to the Book of Confessions*. Philadelphia: Westminster Press, 1985.

———. *Reading the Bible and the Confessions: The Presbyterian Way*. Louisville, KY: Geneva Press, 1999.

Rohls, Jan. *Reformed Confessions: Theology from Zurich to Barmen*. Trans. John Hoffmeyer. Columbia Series in Reformed Theology. Louisville, KY: Westminster John Knox Press, 1997.

Weeks, Louis B. *The Presbyterian Source: Bible Words That Shape a Faith*. Louisville, KY: Westminster John Knox Press, 1990.

———. *To Be a Presbyterian*. Rev. ed. Louisville, KY: Geneva Press, 2010.

CPSIA information can be obtained
at www.ICGtesting.com
Printed in the USA
LVHW02s0815281017
554073LV00007B/88/P